'black & white'

'Positive B colour'

'Negative B black & white'

'Positive B colour'

When using the
colour' with colours
the following

CORPORATE IMAGE

for professional communicators

Amanda Barratt

Batsford

Contents

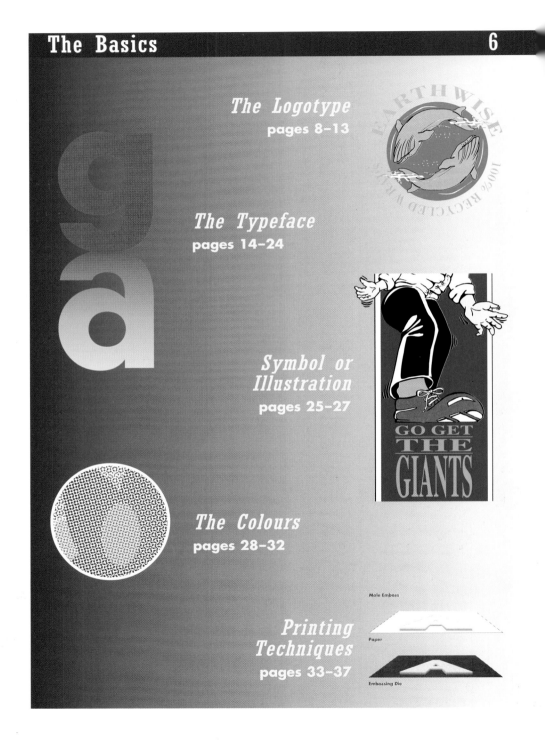

The Basics 6

GO GET
THE
GIANTS

Male Emboss

Paper

Embossing Die

Text and illustrations copyright
© Amanda Barrett
except the following logotypes:
pp8-9 © Virgin Group of Companies,
© University of London, © V.A.G Limited,
© Government of Victoria, Australia.
pp25-27 © Federal Mogul and John
Fletcher & Company, Australia. © Harrison
& Sons Limited, © V.A.G. Limited.
pp58-62 © Government of Victoria,
Australia. © Mercury Holidays Limited, ©
West Suffolk Business Development Centre,
© State Electricity Commission of Australia.

A special thank you to everyone who has
helped with contributions and advice in the
compiling of this book.

ISBN 0 7134 7476 9
A CIP catalogue record for this book is
available from the British Library.

Jacket and title page design by André Jute.
Interior design and typesetting by the
author.

Printed in Singapore for the publisher
B. T. Batsford Ltd
4 Fitzhardinge Street
London W1H 0AH

Identity is central to our world of diverse cultures. It confers a sense of belonging resulting from a complex mix of birthright and choice. Ultimately you choose to associate with, or disassociate from, a particular group – be it social, political or religious. You also choose to use the services of a particular company or buy a specific brand of product. What influences that choice forms the payroll of advertising agencies world-wide. There is no definitive answer, as no one can generalize the experiences of a particular individual – we all have our own identity, and so it should be for the company.

Drawing upon its own expertise, corporate history and knowledge of the market place a company should seek to create its own identity, which is not just expressed graphically but should permeate the whole structure of the organization. As graphic designers we should hold a mirror up to this company structure and create an image that reflects its history and aims. Having formed an image our task is then to 'polish it' – refine it, conferring upon it the advantages of good design, ensuring that the image is memorable, distinctive and long lasting.

The Most Important Marketing Asset a Business can have

No matter what size a company is – whether a multi-national corporation, a charitable organization or an individual trader – the graphic image that the company first presents provides the basis upon which a judgement of its business is formed. It is this image that is the keystone of the corporate identity.

The Keystone of the Corporate Identity: the Logotype

In the first instance, the graphic image presented by a company takes the form of the logotype, appearing on anything from a letterhead or carrier bag to the side of a van or even a plane.

The word logotype has come to mean the symbol, lettering style or combination of both that is used to identify a company or organization. The design of this logo is often undervalued as most people can and do design their own company logo with varying degrees of success. The real test is whether the logo works. Does it present the right image for the company? If trade is slack and enquiries are down to a trickle it could be that the present logo fails to convey a positive corporate image.

A logo can be designed to convey any number of symbolic associations — stable, dependable, formal, progressive, creative, hi-tech — to name but a few. The trick is to convey the *right* image.

For an educational institution a heraldic symbol is ideal, having associations with history and learning.

A memorable name with distinctive typography ensures instant recognition. The Virgin logo portrays a forward thinking company, achieved by the upward angle of the type and the use of an informal style of hand-written lettering.

The initials V and W for Volkswagen were successfully combined to produce this logo which is both distinctive and memorable.

This logo, designed for a Martial Arts and Fitness Centre, draws upon the Japanese origins of the organization. A paintbrush was used to produce both the calligraphy and the illustration.

The architects' plans for a housing development were used as a reference to create this logo. The image was used on banners surrounding the proposed development site as well as appearing on promotional literature.

The Brief

The specific problems facing the designer of a corporate logo have to be solved at the briefing stage. It is essential to get a feel for the company's position in the marketplace along with its aims, potential market and desired client base. This makes the briefing one of the most important stages in the design process.

Some companies may not be able to define the precise image they wish to project and will be looking to the designer for input, while others may have quite clear ideas on their objectives, even to the point of having an actual image in their mind's eye. Both situations call for a comprehensive brief where specific points must be clarified before any design work is started; otherwise a lot of time can be wasted in trying out image after image – eroding the client's confidence in the designer, not to mention the designer's own self esteem!

Key Areas for Discussion

Company Profile
• Company history and background
• Specific services and/or product offered
• Preferred image: e.g. formal, progressive hi-tech etc.

Market
• Who are their competitors and what image do they project.
• Targeted groups for potential clients and/or customers.

Company Structure
• Size of company.
• How many different departments and/or divisions are there? Should there be any graphic differentiation between these?

Reference
Any existing material that can be used as a basis for the logo design:
• photo of premises
• product designs
• tools of the trade
• heraldic devices etc.

Usage
How is the company going to type letters and invoices etc.? Check on their computer facilities and available fonts.
In addition to printed material will the logo be used for:
• uniforms
• vehicle livery
• signage
• packaging etc.

Budget
This will affect your choice of the following:
• quantities
• number of colours
• printing techniques
• paper.

THE COMPANY NAME

Before designing a logotype always check that the client has done a search on the proposed name – i.e. that it has not already been registered by another company.

If the name has not been registered already you can suggest alternative names or modifications to the name, e.g. using only part of an otherwise long name.

Companies dealing abroad should check the name against appropriate foreign languages, just to make sure they are not offending anyone!

Company Profile

A designer must be guided by a company's own analysis of its trading strengths. If the company considers its product or service to be both high in quality and price then the logo should reflect this. Otherwise, potential clients may approach the company asking for prices or even quotations – often a time-consuming exercise – only to find out that the cost is well beyond their expectations and ability to pay.

A logo can reflect a quality service not only through the choice of typeface and overall design but also through the choice of printing technique and grade of paper. An embossed logo on a special paper can look very impressive, but bear in mind how the company stationery will be used. For example, if it is to be put through a laser printer, check that:

● the paper selected and
● the printing process used are suitable for overprinting by a laser printer.

SLOGANS OR STRAP LINES

The use of a phrase or slogan in addition to the logo can define or elaborate upon the company's services/product. However, some phrases or slogans can get you into trouble. For example, claiming that your company is 'the best' or that the service you offer 'cannot be beaten' are not advisable. The ASA (Advertising Standards Association) advises that whatever phrase you use you have to be able to prove it. Obviously claims like 'the best' are impossible to prove (though some notable companies have got round this by inserting the word 'probably' in front of the claim). Likewise, Wellbeck Carpentry could be forced to remove their claim if a client complains that they are neither prompt nor reliable, so beware!

The logos above and opposite show different design solutions for one company.
The corporate image portrayed in the first logo could be described as clean and efficient – an image which is endorsed by the inclusion of the phrase 'prompt reliable service'. In contrast, the second logo has a traditional feel – suggesting a more specialist service.

Design Ideas

Having discussed the job during the course of the design briefing it often becomes obvious what theme a logo design will follow. On the other hand, you can be faced with a blank sheet of paper or an empty computer screen. If it is the latter, try looking through some design magazines. It helps to build up your own reference library and to keep updating it regularly. Use the magazines for ideas only – never be tempted to crib designs. For not only are you infringing copyright, but a logo design is unique and company specific. One company's image is definitely another company's poison!

Design Roughs

Pencil roughs are absolutely essential, even if the final design will be done on computer. It can be slow to build up an initial idea using a keyboard and this also lures the designer into polishing up a single design rather than looking at other options.

When you have found a design solution that shows promise, moving to a computer will help to develop the design and modify it. Exploring colour combinations and finalising the choice of typeface is easier on screen. Output to a colour photocopier or printer will also give a full colour visual for the client to approve.

The final visuals for presentation to the client should be as close as possible to the finished job. If access to a computer is not possible, the specific typeface and colours can be hand drawn. Alternatively, dry transfer lettering, e.g. Letraset©, can be used to render accurately certain typefaces.

These designs are for a manufacturer of gift wrap and gift cards who prints exclusively on recycled paper. The RESY symbol is used as a starting point for the design which gradually evolves into the final decorative logotype shown opposite. The gift wrap design was inspired by the logo.

Choice of Typeface

Like hairstyles, typefaces can be a matter of personal taste or current trend. The skill in selecting a face for a logo lies in matching the face to the company image without offending your own subjective preferences.

Points to consider when choosing a typeface are set out opposite.

Availability
• Unique typeface – logo less likely to be confused with any competitor's.
• Common typeface – allows easier reproduction and text setting can be matched to the logo, particularly if the typeface is available on most PCs.

Usage
Will the typeface be used for the logo only or will it be used for other items as well e.g.
• Forms
• Brochures
• Signage.

Personality
Does the typeface reflect the right image for the company.

Weight
• Light
• Medium
• Bold
If you are going to reverse a typeface out of a background colour you may need a heavier cut of the typeface e.g. bold. Similarly, the colour you are using may affect your choice of typeface.

Reproduction
Will it reproduce cleanly from small sizes:
• Newspaper adverts, through to large sizes:
• Signage
• Vehicle livery etc?

Special Effects
• Hand-drawn
• Computer generated
• Montage
Is it legible and will it reproduce clearly?

TYPEFACE • ROMAN • ITALIC • BOLD • LIGHT • CAPITALS • LOWER CASE • POINT SIZE • LEADING • ALIGNMENT • TYPE EFFECT • COLOUR • PRINTING

If you choose to use a currently popular or trendy typeface be aware of the risk that your logo might date quickly. However, this might not matter in industries where the 'look' of the 60s or 90s might be their main aim, or with industries that regularly up-date their corporate image, such as the fashion industry.

Each typeface has its own personality and history. For example, Fette Fraktur is a serif typeface derived from the gothic faces used in German Medieval manuscripts. It strongly evokes the feeling of age and history, used on European pub signs, church notice boards and any product wishing to convey a feeling of tradition and antiquity.

The White Hart

A much lighter personality can be attributed to this modern script face — Freestyle Script. The characters are loosely drawn and have a lively feel; they seem to bounce along the baseline rather than sit upon it. This face belongs to the growing group of decorative typefaces which have become increasingly popular since the Second World War.

Life is a Beach!

Times New Roman was designed as a result of the Times newspaper asking Stanley Morison to create a typeface specifically for newspaper work. It first appeared in the Times on the 3 October 1932. Being based upon the old-style serif typefaces Times has a classical feel, its personality is authoritative, and is in complete contrast to the frivolous Freestyle Script illustrated above.

Times New Roman is easy to read as text setting, it is also suitable for display sizes –

like this heading in 48 pt size type.

Serif Typefaces

ABCDEFGHIJ
KLMNOPQR
STUVWXYZ
abcdefghijklmn
opqrstuvwxyz
0123456789

BODONI

BODONI BOLD

BODONI BOLD ITALIC

Serif

Ascender

BODONI ITALIC

ABCDEFGHIJ
KLMNOPQR
STUVWXYZ
abcdefghijklmn
opqrstuvwxyz
0123456789

TIMES NEW ROMAN

Serifs

TIMES ITALIC

TIMES BOLD

The finishing strokes at the ends of the characters are known as serifs. The two main categories of typefaces are those with serifs and those without – 'sans' serif. The typefaces within these categories are really families of typefaces sharing a common name. For example, Bodoni, which first appeared in Italy around 1800, has been added to over the years to include bold, bold italic and poster. Some of these family members are shown here in colour alongside their parents.

ABCDEFGHIJ
KLMNOPQR
STUVWXYZ
abcdefghijklmn
opqrstuvwxyz
0123456789

Slab Serif

Slab Serif

LUBALIN GRAPH

Sans Serif Typefaces

ABCDEFGHIJ
KLMNOPQR
STUVWXYZ
abcdefghijklmn
opqrstuvwxyz
0123456789

HELVETICA

The first sans serif typefaces to appear in England arrived in the early 1800s. However, Futura did not appear until 1928, and Helvetica, in various weights, from 1957-59. Helvetica (originally called Neue Haas Grotesk) has a very large family which can cause some confusion. Always check that the typeface you have used is the same one that your output bureau holds, or you could find your carefully typeset documents re-flowing or missing pieces of text.

ERAS BOOK

ABCDEFGHIJ
KLMNOPQR
STUVWXYZ
abcdefghijklmn
opqrstuvwxyz
0123456789

FUTURA BOOK

ABCDEFGHIJ
KLMNOPQR
STUVWXYZ
abcdefghijklmn
opqrstuvwxyz
0123456789

Descender

Typesetting

The variety of typefaces and special effects that can be seen in printed literature today owes a lot to the advances in computer technology. Previously typefaces had been set in hot metal – a medium which physically limited the ways in which type could be manipulated. Although the hot metal process has now been superseded by modern technology, the terminology and the methods used to measure and categorize typefaces remain the same.

Normal
100%

150%

Set Width

Literally the width at which a character has been set. This can be adjusted by increasing or reducing the horizontal scale.

Type Size

The size of a typeface is measured in points: 72pt = 1in. The example opposite is in 90pt Goudy, the type size is measured from *just above* the top of the ascender to *just below* the base of the descender. This is to ensure that when the type is set solid – with no leading, the ascenders and descenders do not touch each other.

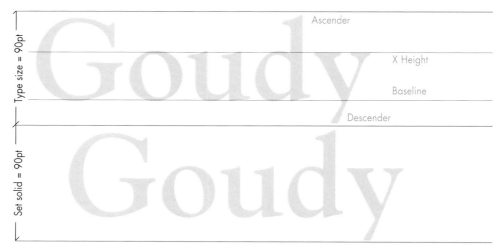

Type size = 90pt

Set solid = 90pt

Ascender

X Height

Baseline

Descender

Goudy

Goudy

For body text the general rule governing the use of leading is that it should be 20% of the type size. The 'auto' setting for leading on most computer fonts is set at this percentage. This text has been set in 10pt Times with 2pt leading, so it is using the 20% rule. 10/12pt Times New Roman.

However, you may feel that text looks better with a bit more space: an additional 2pt, perhaps? The only real rule governing leading on body text is to ensure it is easy to read. 10/14pt Times New Roman

When type is set solid it becomes difficult to read especially over a long line length, sometimes causing you to skip a line as you read. Also, the body copy tends to look very black which can be off-putting for the reader. 10/10pt Times New Roman or Times New Roman set solid

Leading

This name is derived from the strips of lead that were inserted between the lines of metal type to increase the inter-line spacing. The shorthand used to express type size and amount of leading is size of type/sum of the type size + the amount of leading.

THIS HEADING IN 30PT TIMES NEW ROMAN IS SET ON 26PT LEADING

It is also possible to have leading set with a value less than the type size: e.g. some headings set all in capitals look too spaced out set solid and a minus figure is preferable.

Tracking

This allows you to adjust the spacing between selected words and characters. It can be used as a copyfitting tool, e.g. to reduce the tracking when a line is too long by a character, or use it decoratively to improve the look of headings and to open up space in text. However, be careful not to overdo it – the third line in the text sample shown is far too closely spaced.

Tracking can be used to o p e n u p t y p e o r close up type to fit this space. You can also do this with l e t t e r s p a c i n g

Kerning

This is used when you want to reduce space between individual characters and it is particularly useful on large type sizes. The space has been reduced between the 'O' and the 'V' and the 'V' and the 'E' on the lower word shown opposite.

BASELINE SHIFT

+15

Baseline

– 8

Baseline Shift

Adjust the baseline of individual characters to fall above or below the standard baseline.

Type Alignment

Type aligned on the left is easier to read than type aligned right, so for quantities of text it is better to avoid the align right option.

A variety of text effects are possible using a combination of leading, spacing and alignment. This paragraph has been set in Goudy 11pt with 3pt leading. The tracking has been set to give wide inter-letter spacing whilst the type has been aligned left.

Ranged or Aligned Left

See the difference when this paragraph is aligned on the right. You begin to notice the overall shape of the text. It is still set in Goudy 11pt with 3pt leading. Do you find this more difficult to read than the text that is aligned left?

Ranged Right or Aligned Right

Now this paragraph is centred, and the overall shape of the text is symmetrical. The shape is very important and by breaking lines up into shorter or longer lines you can manipulate the final shape.

Centred

A justified paragraph is straight on both sides of the text. It is a good idea to use hyphenation with justified text or you will end up with large gaps between the words.

Hyphenation together with minimum and max-imum word/letter spacing can be adjusted to suit your needs in most DTP programs.

Justified

Column width = 94mm or 22.5picas

All the examples on this page have been set to the same column width of 94 mm. Sometimes picas (1 pica =12pts) are used as a unit of measurement.

By experimenting you can create some interesting effects for selective use on otherwise boring blocks of text!

For extra interest a bold italic drop cap has been added to this text ✦ The font Zapf Dingbats has been used to provide a decorative symbol to replace the normal full stops ✦ While the horizontal scale of the text has been increased to 140% the typeface remains the same, it is still typeset in 11pt Goudy with 3pt leading ✦ The tracking has been increased to open up the text ✦ Overall the effect is strikingly different from the text samples shown opposite ✦

—— Column width = 94mm or 22.5picas ——

5mm Gutter

Most desktop publishing programs will let you specify a drop cap. The size of the drop cap is initially determined by the amount of lines you specify for the drop. Some programs will then let you amend the size and type style of the drop cap if desired. The cap used at the start of this copy is a hanging drop cap 3 lines deep. By entering a command to indent the text before the second character in this paragraph the drop cap has been forced to hang in the newly created left indent margin.

Another technique is to drop in a character as a separate graphic element and specify the stand-off area for the text to runaround. This allows you to customize your drop cap and to position it where you like. Some programs allow you to adjust the runaround area to form irregular shapes. In this instance the 'f' has been imported as a picture from a draw program. The runaround is then added automatically to the edges of the image by selecting auto image from the runaround specifications.

Runaround Text

By inserting a graphic in the centre of these two columns of text and setting the runaround area, you can force text to flow around an object.

—— Column width = 61mm or 14.4picas —— —— Column width = 45mm or 10.6picas ——

Type Effects

After selecting a suitable typeface for a logotype, the next stage is to assess at what size, degree of spacing etc. you are going to use it. The effectiveness of how a word communicates lies in the way it portrays its meaning. Type effects should be used to emphasize this meaning as well as to give aesthetic form to the words. It is very easy to fall into the trap of using type effects for their decorative value only at the expense of legibility. First sketch out an idea that works on paper, then try to find the best means of reproducing it on the computer. If along the way you discover a good type effect – great – but remember some of the best logotypes are also the simplest.

Envelope Effects
Used judiciously envelopes can squeeze and distort type to good effect. The two examples shown right were set in Times New Roman and Helvetica Bold.

Horizontal Scale
This sample has been set in Times Bold, the size of the typeface measured in points is as follows: 24pt horizontally scaled to 145%, 32pt scaled by 195% and 120pt scaled by 30% respectively. The leading has been adjusted to fit the lines closely together.

BRILLIANT

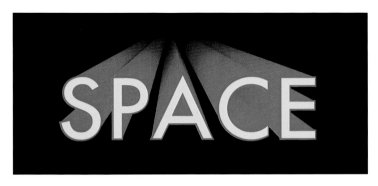

SPACE

Zoom Effect

Created using a type effect available on some draw programs. The yellow type with blue outlines is a clone of the blue type before the zoom effect was applied. It has been brought to the front obscuring the blue type underneath.

Converting Type To Paths (not to be confused with *joining* type to paths, see below) allows you to manipulate individual letters of a type face, changing their shape and adding effects like the Neon example shown above.

How To Create Neon Type
Using Aldus FreeHand

■ Type letters in 60pt Futura Bold and space to allow for width of neon effect (12pt).

■ Convert to paths, go to Element menu, select split element, then select split element again, tab to deselect.

■ Select the counters of the 'B' and drag clear of character outline. Clone character outline and set line in 12pt black and fill black, then send to back.

■ Tab and re-select 1st 'B' outline, set 1pt line in white and fill in black, tab to deselect.

counters

■ Drag select a pair of corresponding points – see diagram (they do not highlight when selected).

■ Blend (10 steps)

■ Select fill only on colour palette, choose desired colour.

■ **For counters only,** select one, scale to 15%, clone, set line in 12pt white, fill black, send to back and deselect. Re-select 1st counter, set line in 0.5pt black, fill white. Blend lines as described above, then select fill only and colour black.

■ Repeat for all letters and colour background black. Group and Save.

Joining Text To Paths

Some programs will allow you to join text to paths. In this case a semi-circle is drawn and then selected together with the type – News Gothic. The two are then joined to form one element.

JOINING TEXT TO A PATH IS AN INCREASINGLY POPULAR EFFECT

Patterned Line

counter

line pattern 6pt wide

■ Type 'g' in 100pt Futura Medium.
■ Convert to paths.
■ Go to Fill and Line under Attributes, select desired colour fill, and line pattern as shown.
■ Go to Element menu, select Split elements then deselect element.
■ Re-select individual points, move to manipulate line.
■ Bring the counter to front, set in white line and fill.

Emboss Effect

■ Colours used are: Light Blue = 20% cyan, 10% yellow. Green = 30% cyan, 30% yellow. Grey = 40% cyan, 20% magenta, 40% yellow.
■ Type 'g' in 100pt Futura Bold, colour in Light Blue.
■ Clone the 'g'.
■ Select Move: Horizontal 0.5mm, Vertical minus 0.5mm, colour Green.
■ Clone again and move by same settings (or duplicate for same result), colour Grey, send to back.
■ Fill the background in Green.

Patterned Fill

■ Type 'g' in Futura Bold.
■ Convert to paths.
■ Go to Fill and Line, select patterned under Fill, click on choice, set colour set Line at 0.5pt.
NOTE: patterned fills always reproduce at the same size no matter how an element is scaled or saved.

Reflection

■ Colours used are: Red = 90% magenta, 60% yellow. Orange = 20% magenta 40% yellow
■ Type 'g' in 100pt Futura Bold, colour Red.
■ Clone the 'g'.
■ Select Reflection tool, click horizontal axis.
■ Convert reflected 'g' to paths.
■ Go to Attributes. Set fill to graduated and angle to 270°, select linear from Red to Orange.

Radial Fill

■ Colours used are: Light Blue = 30% cyan Turquoise = 30% cyan 10% yellow. Purple = 80% cyan, 60% magenta 10% yellow.
■ Type 'g' in Futura Bold.
■ Convert to paths.
■ Go to Fill and Line select Radial under Fill, Turquoise to Purple.
■ Split element, select outlines and set to Light Blue.

All the examples shown above were made using Aldus FreeHand.

A company logo can use a typographic element on its own or complement the typography with a symbol or illustration.

For high profile industries whose client/customer base is drawn from the general public, the more memorable the company logo the better. Using an illustration in addition to the company namestyle can be an attractive solution. It can also help to identify the premises of a business – this is particularly useful for restaurants and public houses.

The 'Go Get the Giants' logo was designed for an incentive campaign, the objective being to motivate the sales force of a company to help them achieve certain sales targets. As participation in the scheme was voluntary, the logo was designed to be both intriguing and exciting to encourage enrolment in the scheme.

An illustration is used to add interest and humanize this logo. The head of the figure was deliberately cut off to keep its identity anonymous as it represents one of the 'Giants' – the big buyers targeted in the company incentive campaign.

This logo is made up from a rough pen and ink drawing of the premises, which was scanned and saved in TIFF format. The type was set in Times Bold. By resizing the vowels and using baseline shift it was possible to align all the characters at cap height. 'Thatched Cottage' was filled in beige and given an outline in burgundy. Finally the TIFF image was placed in position and scaled to fit the required width.

A symbol is a graphic device that can signify a number of associations. Perhaps the most well known examples of the use of symbols are posted along our roads – the signs that constitute the Highway Code. It is easier to remember and comprehend a simple visual image than written instructions, particularly when they are seen only fleetingly.

Similarly, a company symbol will be retained in the mind more readily than a long company name. It also has the advantage of being able to elicit any number of desired associations which makes it a very useful tool.

Phonetic Association

The first of these associations could be phonetic. A symbol can be used that has the same sound as the company name or part of the company name e.g. Robin for Robinson. A colour can also be used in this way e.g. Red for Redman.

Literal Association

This is a popular use of symbolism. The company initials are used as the basis for the logo design. Many well known companies have used this device so successfully, that the initials are used as a verbal short hand in preference to the full company name.

The highly memorable Volkswagen logotype is an example of strong design using literal association.

The printer's trademark, which is the symbol for the high security printers Harrison & Sons Ltd, dates back to the 16th Century. It is a good example of phonetic association depicting a hare, a sheaf of rye and the sun – or Har-ri-son. The symbol used by the company today incorporates the date 1562.

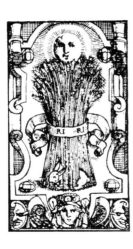

Profession/Product Association

Sometimes it is not obvious from the company name what type of business the company is involved in. A symbol can be used to define the area of its operation. In the case of the manufacturing and retailing industries, a symbol can be used to define the product range, or the attributes of a specific product.

Abstract/Decorative Association

A symbol can be used primarily as a decorative feature but it will still signify certain relevant information about the company. A very bright splash of colour would be interpreted differently from a neat rectangle of the same colour.
A decorative symbol could be made up of several parts, each symbolizing a different division of the company or the key individuals like those that form a business partnership.

These are some of the most common ways of using symbols as part of a corporate identity, though they are by no means definitive – symbols can have several associations and may not fit snugly into one category.

This symbol, based upon the shape of a rainbow, is used for a manufacturer who specializes in lights that closely match the spectrum of natural daylight.

In this logotype, below, each partner is indicated by the use of a different colour. The three colours then combine to form the eye symbol.

Newell, Bennet & Cole

O P T I C I A N S

Choice of Colours

Some products or organizations are synonymous with certain colours – e.g red for Coca-Cola, white and light blue for the United Nations. There are very practical reasons for this strong colour branding. A Coke tin stands out on a supermarket shelf. The white UN vehicles are deliberately conspicuous to avoid inadvertent attacks.

A distinctive colour can identify a company or product as readily as a name, but it also has the advantage of signifying different moods and associations, such as for the UN white, which was chosen to signify peace.

Effect of Other Colours
• Colours on top of different backgrounds
• Colours reversing out of other colours

Reproduction Process
How is it going to be reproduced?
• Printed paper
• Signage
• Clothing – T shirts, overalls, uniforms
• Photocopying

Cost
This will be affected by:
• Number of colours
• Type of colour – Pantone or Process

Monochrome
Single colour version of a coloured logo
• How well will it reproduce
• Use of tints

Pantone or Process Colours
• What to use when
• Specifying colours

Paper
Your choice of the following will affect colour reproduction
• Uncoated paper
• Coated paper
• Tinted Paper

Cost

There are several factors that will affect your choice of colours for a logotype and company stationery. The chart on the opposite page outlines the key points to consider.

As most designs have to be produced within a restricted budget, the first question to ask yourself is how many colours can you afford. It is pointless designing a multi-coloured logotype needing four individual printing plates if the final printing cost is prohibitive.

Process Colour

There are two main types of printed colour:

● Four Colour Process (CMYK)
● Pantone Colour System

Process colour is used primarily to print documents containing coloured photographs or illustrations. This book, for example, is printed in process colours. The four process colours are:

cyan

magenta

yellow

black (or key)

Each of the four process colours are printed from a separate printing plate.

Colour photographs and illustrations are scanned to break them down into four separate images – separations – one for each process colour. Each separation is a screened image made up of dots – large dots where the ink must be dense and small dots where it is thin. When printed one on top of the other the four separations optically combine to produce any colour required (with the exception of metallic colours which require special inks).

By looking at the magnified section of the illustration, it is easy to see the dots making up each colour separation.

Process colour is generally not suitable for the reproduction of a corporate logotype on company stationery — unless you wish to reproduce a full colour illustration or photograph.

The use of four colour process can be an expensive option. Many jobs can be printed in two colours if Pantone colours are used instead.

Using process colours, four printing plates – cyan, magenta, yellow and black – are required to print the Thatched Cottage logo shown below.

Cyan separation.   Magenta separation.

Yellow separation.   Black separation.

Note how the fine lines in the illustration are broken up by the screen used to produce the tints of the relevant process colours. If the colours are misregistered then these lines will become blurred.

Pantone Colours

Pantone colours differ from process colours in that they are mixed prior to printing. You can select any colour from the Pantone range and print it as solid colour. It is not screened unless you specifically ask for a tint of that colour.

The advantages of using Pantone colours are:
● Economy
● Colour quality

We have already seen how the Thatched Cottage logo requires four printing plates when reproducing it in process colours. When the same image is reproduced using Pantone colours it requires only two:
● Pantone 465 (the beige)
● Pantone 506 (the burgundy)

Using Pantone colours, the image is reproduced using solid colour apart from the use of a 50% tint of 506 (burgundy) on the rules under the cottage and main heading. By using solid colour the quality of the fine lines are preserved and problems of misregistration lessened.

Note: we have simulated the Pantone colours shown above as we are limited to process colours for the reproduction of this book. You will not be able to see the improvement in quality that would be evident with Pantone colours.

How will it Look?

Three key elements affect the way a colour reproduces:

1. Type of paper.

Glossy papers – coated papers, will intensify a colour, giving it a glossy sheen. Matt papers – uncoated papers, e.g. laid paper, have the opposite effect and tend to darken the colour. The difference in colour can be quite dramatic and it is for this reason that Pantone colour swatch books have two sets of colours ones printed on Coated paper (having a 'C' after their reference number), and those printed on Uncoated paper (having a 'U').

Initially, a logo may just be reproduced on company stationery using uncoated paper, however, later on it may be used in a full colour glossy (coated paper) brochure which will be printed in process colours. When specifying process colour tints to match the Pantone colours printed on the company stationery, bear in mind the effect that the change of paper will have on the colour.

2. Paper colour.

Obviously a tinted paper will dramatically affect the way a colour prints.

3. Other colours.

Colours are influenced by the colours surrounding them. When using coloured type against a background colour, make sure that there is sufficient contrast between the two colours. Avoid using light typefaces against background colours as any misregistration will reduce legibility.

When applying colour to type, if the area of colour is small, you will need to adjust the density of the colour to suit the background.

Opposite: Tints of the process colours at 10%, 30%, 60% and 100% are shown against a variety of coloured backgrounds.

When viewing colours on a computer screen the shades displayed are not necessarily how the colours will look when printed. A computer screen can only simulate printed colour – its own mode of display is through Red, Green and Blue light. *Always* check your selected colour against a process chart or Pantone colour swatch.

Monochrome

When preparing artwork for the monochrome version of a logo, bear in mind how it is going to be used.

Three key elements affect the clarity of reproduction:

1. Method of printing (see Printing Techniques page 33). Some processes cannot handle small type and fine screens.

2. Quality of paper. Fine paper (papers with a very smooth finish) will accept a small dot screen e.g. 133 – 150 lines per inch. Coarse papers, such as those used in trade directories and newspapers, need a larger dot screen e.g. 60 – 90lpi.

3. Typeface. The style, the size and the background the type is set against will affect the quality of reproduction.

On the right are samples of different screens. The type, set in Helvetica at various sizes, acts as a guide to what will reproduce well and – what won't.

Make up your own screen samples with your chosen typeface – black on and reversed out of the different screened backgrounds – as a guide to reproduction. The screens shown opposite were made up in Aldus FreeHand. Boxes were drawn and filled in the different percentages of black then the halftone screen was selected from under the Attributes menu. Screen Type – default, Screen Angle – 45° and the Screen Rulings – 65lpi, 100lpi and 133lpi respectively. The type was then set in Helvetica, one sample in black and one in white. Output your samples as film positives using a trade bureau.

65 lpi screen

6pt 7pt 8pt 10pt 12pt
15% Black

6pt 7pt 8pt 10pt 12pt
30% Black

6pt 7pt 8pt 10pt 12pt
45% Black

6pt 7pt 8pt 10pt 12pt
60% Black

6pt 7pt 8pt 10pt 12pt
75% Black

6pt 7pt 8pt 10pt 12pt
90% Black

100 lpi screen

6pt 7pt 8pt 10pt 12pt
15% Black

6pt 7pt 8pt 10pt 12pt
30% Black

6pt 7pt 8pt 10pt 12pt
45% Black

6pt 7pt 8pt 10pt 12pt
60% Black

6pt 7pt 8pt 10pt 12pt
75% Black

6pt 7pt 8pt 10pt 12pt
90% Black

133 lpi screen

6pt 7pt 8pt 10pt 12pt
15% Black

6pt 7pt 8pt 10pt 12pt
30% Black

6pt 7pt 8pt 10pt 12pt
45% Black

6pt 7pt 8pt 10pt 12pt
60% Black

6pt 7pt 8pt 10pt 12pt
75% Black

6pt 7pt 8pt 10pt 12pt
90% Black

While designing a logotype, it is as well to keep in mind how the final job will be printed as it will affect the way you prepare the artwork.

Printing 'In House'

Most companies now have sophisticated computer equipment and may wish to generate their own stationery. Find out what their requirements are before designing the logo. Laser printers are often used to overprint stationery that has already been printed by litho.

Take special care when choosing a paper for a company letterhead, as some laid and textured papers do not print well when run through a laser printer – sometimes the powder does not fix properly and can flake off. Test a sample of the paper through a laser printer before committing yourself, and obtain the manufacturer's guarantee that the paper is suitable for use with laser printers.

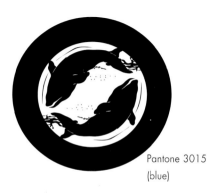

Pantone 3015
(blue)

Black

Pantone 271
(purple)

To produce the logo shown left in three Pantone colours, colour-separated artwork is required.

These separations should be presented on film and generally in negative as shown below.

Lithography

This is the most commonly used method of printing for company stationery, brochures and promotional literature.

Lithography is the method by which a printing plate is treated with a photo-sensitive coating which is then exposed to the image of artwork from the colour-separated film. After the image has been properly fixed within the surface of the plate it is inked up, transferring the image via a rubber roller (hence the term 'offset' litho) to the paper. The result is a thin film of ink lying on the paper. You are looking at this result now! It is the method used for printing this book.

The top image is scanned at 300dpi, simulating the quality of an image output on a laser printer at this resolution, the ragged edges to the letters are clearly visible. The middle image simulates the quality of an image output at 600dpi. Contrast this with the bottom image which was output at a resolution of over 1200dpi.

1234abcd

1234abcd

1234abcd

USING COMMERCIAL OUTPUT BUREAUS
check list

■ Can they handle IBM/Apple Macintosh etc, (whichever is applicable)?

■ Do they have a copy of the program and relevant version that you have used?

■ Do they have the typefaces you have used? Send them a record of all the different typefaces that you have used in the document. Note: It is possible to save a file in EPS format which can be output on a postscript printer without the fonts you used; however, check this with the bureau. Remember that any last minute corrections needed to an EPS file are difficult if not impossible for the bureau to do – you will have to do them yourself.

■ Do you require bromide or film output? Note the size and whether or not to include crop marks (and registration marks for colour separated work).

■ For films specify negative or positive and right or wrong reading, if in doubt consult your printer.

■ Always send a hard copy e.g. laser print (of the latest version!) of the job along with the disk.

■ Always keep a master copy of your job in case of disk failure.

■ Finally, if you are in any doubt ASK.

Artwork requirements

Any of the following can be used as line artwork:

● Black and white laser print out of image. It is not advisable to use this for lithographic reproduction if your laser printer has a resolution of less than 600dpi because the edges of an image will look ragged at a lower resolution.

● Black and white bromide. This should be marked up for colour if applicable.

● Film, usually negatives, colour separated if applicable.

● Image on computer disk.

Check with your printer as to which of the above is most suitable/economic.

For artwork containing photographs or illustrations, (not generated on the computer), the images will have to be scanned separately and combined with the line artwork either on the computer or at film stage. For a quality result this is best done through the printer or output bureau.

Many designers will supply laser prints to a client for approval. These will be either black and white or full colour depending on the job. Once these are approved the computer disk containing the image will be sent to an output bureau. The bureau will run out either bromides or film as directed by the designer. It is essential to make sure that the bureau has all the relevant information in order to output the job correctly. A check list is shown opposite, but do not hesitate to ask both your printer and the bureau for specific advice.

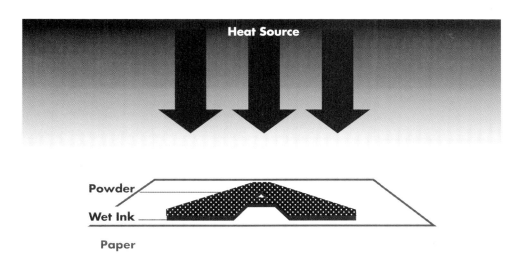

Heat Source

Powder

Wet Ink

Paper

This cross-section shows the raised finish that is produced through thermography.

A variety of powders are available for different effects, ranging from a glossy to a pearl sheen and from solid colours (including gold and silver) to translucent colours which can have glitter added to them.

Thermography

This produces a raised image. It uses a conventional process initially to print the paper, then, while the ink is still wet it is sprinkled with a powder which on exposure to heat melts and expands. When dry the thermography is hard but not brittle.

Two points to remember are:
● This process will thicken up an image. Fine typefaces will tend to 'fill in'.
● Until recently you could not run thermographed stationery through a laser printer as this would melt the thermography. Now a new powder has been developed which is cured by UV light and is safe for use with laser printers.

Artwork requirements

Line artwork as for litho.
Avoid using large dense areas of thermography alongside finer details as the increased temperature used to melt the

large area will cause the finer detail to spread and 'fill-in'.

This process is not suitable for photographic halftone images, but can be used successfully on line illustrations.

Silkscreen

This versatile process allows you to print on a range of materials including perspex and fabrics. Not economical for jobs requiring long print runs it is often used for posters and signage where the amount of copies required are in the hundreds rather than the thousands.

As the printing ink is forced through a fine mesh screen, the minimum type size and thickness of line is determined by the fineness of the screen.

Artwork requirements

As for litho. Consult your printer to determine the minimum size typeface and line weight before preparing final artwork.

Embossing

With this technique you can have a raised or recessed image. It can be used in conjunction with litho printing, embossing a previously printed image so that it stands out from the paper. Alternatively, it can be used 'blind' where the paper is embossed without the printed colour.

Left: A male emboss raises the surface of the paper, while below, a female emboss produces a recessed image. In each case the reverse of the paper will be affected.

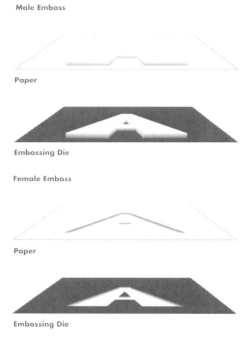

Male Emboss

Paper

Embossing Die

Female Emboss

Paper

Embossing Die

Two points to remember are:
● The reverse side of the paper where it has been embossed will be affected. If you wish to print both sides of a sheet bear this in mind.
● Overprinting embossed stationery with a laser or ink jet printer will flatten the effect, and may cause problems with the paper jamming the printer.

Artwork requirements

As for litho, but the image that is to be embossed must allow the paper or card to be pressed down between letters and/or shapes – avoid small gaps and fine type.

Check that the paper you select is suitable for embossing.

Foil Blocking or Hot Foil

A gloss or matt metallic effect can be achieved through the use of this technique. A metal film is used instead of printing ink. It is bonded to the paper with heat and pressure. As with the embossing process the reverse of the paper or card can be affected.

Artwork requirements

As for litho. Not suitable for overprinting by laser printers.

Die Cutting (Forme Cutting)

Anything requiring an irregular cut out shape must be die cut. This includes folders, boxes, fancy cards, point of sale items and jigsaws etc.

A die or forme is a plate with a raised cutting edge. It is the shape of this edge that determines the area to be cut out (or perforated). The printed sheet is run over the forme which through the application of pressure cuts the sheet to the desired shape. Perforations are achieved by using the same method, the solid cutting edge being replaced with a perforating edge.

If, for example, you are designing a box you would prepare the artwork according to the print process being used but in

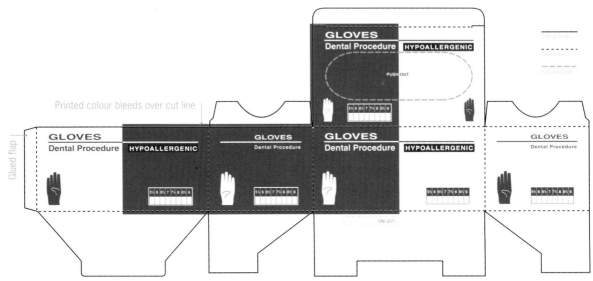

Printed colour bleeds over cut line

Glued flap

Flaps at base of box lock together when assembled.

addition to that artwork you would also supply a keyline master of the shape of the box before it is assembled. Some printers are most obliging over this and will give you a guide for the forme themselves — obtain this before preparing artwork so you know the exact shape you have to work with. It is possible to use existing formes that the printer holds. This saves on cost as you don't have to have one specially made up. Consult your printer!

Artwork requirements
A separate piece of artwork is required from which the die will be made.

Flexography
Used for the printing of packaging and wrappings where long print runs are required. It is particularly suitable for printing on plastics and highly absorbent surfaces such as tissue paper (e.g. paper serviettes) and corrugated boxes. Carrier bags are often printed by this method, (alternatively, silkscreen printing is used).

Artwork requirements
Depending on the type of press the printer uses and the substrate that he is printing on you will have to allow for grip between colours. This can often be as much as 1–2 mm. Consult with your printer before preparing artwork for this process.

Above: A die cut box showing the shape of the cutting forme (or die). The designer should always cut out and fold up a copy of the artwork to check fit before printing and die cutting as mistakes are costly.

Left: The grip (also known as trapping in lithography) is increased in flexography to help colour registration. The top image has no grip and shows what happens when the two colours mis-register. The bottom image has a grip of 1mm which overprints the lighter background colour.

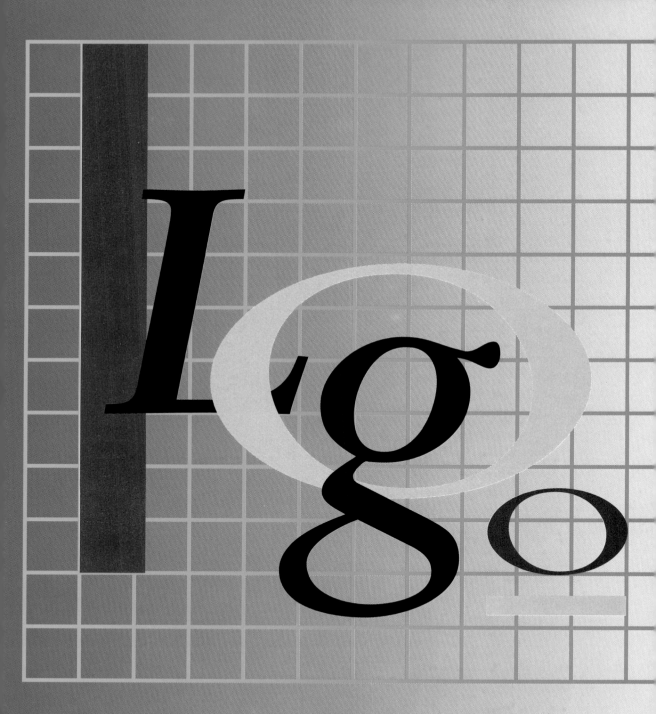

As a company expands and grows, many different individuals and departments will assume responsibility for the production of literature for both internal and external use, from forms through to glossy brochures. In addition there may be requirements for other items — vehicle livery, signage, uniforms and packaging. Anything that is produced by, or on behalf of, the company should reflect the corporate image.

It is the function of the corporate style manual to set out guidelines to ensure that the image presented by the company is consistent, and the logotype — the basis of the corporate image — should be protected from misuse. Initially a style manual may take the form of guidelines governing the correct usage of the company logo on stationery. For large companies however, the guidelines may cover many applications.

The successful style manual is a 'living' document updated and added to as the needs of a company grow and develop. It should allow the company to produce some material 'in house' as well as providing all the relevant information for outside designers.

The following pages are in the form of a basic style manual for a fictitious company, with additional notes on how to produce various items. In practice it is up to the individual company working with designers to define the precise areas to be covered by the corporate style manual.

Important Note:

Due to the format of this book it is not possible to show the following examples of stationery at the correct size. In a style manual it is essential that these items should appear at their printed size. Our examples are shown at approximately 57%, however, all the measurements and type specifications are for the full sized documents.

CREATE A DIGITAL STYLE MANUAL

■ Draw and save master copies of a logo in a format that can be imported into both database and DTP programs.

■ Copy the logo to the computer's scrapbook or clipboard for easy access when working on new projects.

■ Set up templates for stationery items, newsletters and brochures etc. By doing this you save a master copy that cannot inadvertently be overwritten or modified.

■ Compile sample pages on how to use a logo with examples of what will reproduce well and what to avoid.

Some of the leading international companies have now digitized their corporate style manuals, making them available on CD Rom. The corporate image is instantly accessible to authorised departments. This allows simple updates to existing stationery designs to be made 'in house', while at the same time providing all the information an outside design studio needs to produce new work.

Warning: <u>Never</u> hand out digitized copies of a company logo without finding out, a) what it is to be used for, b) sanctioning its use for the specified purpose only, and, c) sending the relevant style guidelines for that specific usage.

Colour 'A' Version of the Logotype

The 'Positive A colour' version of the logotype is shown right. There is no 'Negative A colour' version of the logo. Where the logo is to appear against dark backgrounds the 'Positive B colour' (panel version) should be used.

Bleed

Background grid shows the correct proportions and positioning of logo elements only and should not be reproduced.

Monochrome 'A' Versions of the Logotype

'Positive A' uses: 60% black on the vertical bar and small 'o' 30% black on large 'o' and horizontal bar.

'Negative A' uses:- 30% black on the vertical bar and small 'o' 50% black on large 'o' and horizontal bar. The letters 'L' and 'g' reverse out white.

'Positive A monochrome'

'Negative A monochrome'

Monochrome and Colour 'B' Versions (Panel Versions) of the Logotype

The grid is used to define the panel size and position of the logo and does not reproduce. The 'Positive B colour' version of the logo can have a panel colour other than white if it is selected from the colours listed right.

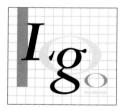

'Positive B monochrome'

'Positive B colour'

'Negative B monochrome'

'Positive B colour'

There are two main versions of the logotype used by Fictitious Logo Limited:

● **'A' Versions** – where the logotype is reproduced in monochrome or colour *without* a panel.

● **'B' Versions** – where the logotype is reproduced in monochrome or colour *within* a panel.

These two versions are subdivided into positive and negative forms for both the monochrome and colour logotypes, with the exception of the colour logotype 'A version' which has a positive form only.

Colours

The colour version of the logotype is achieved in 2-colour line printing by using the Pantone Matching System and specifying the following:

Red: PMS 1795.
Black: Pantone Process Black
Grey: 30% tint of Process Black

For four colour process printing the following tints should be specified:

Red: 100% magenta + 100% yellow
Black: 100% black
Grey: 30% black

When using the version 'Positive B colour' with a panel colour other than white, the colour chosen must match one of the following:

Pantone 3015
Pantone 3145
Pantone 3278
Pantone 121
Pantone 155

Protecting the Logo

The logo must always be reproduced in a two-dimensional, undistorted form. It must not be set at an angle. No part of the logo should be added to or removed.

The logo must be positioned to allow the red vertical bar to bleed from either:-
a. the top of the printed page, or
b. the top of the panel box.
Under no circumstances should this bar be extended or reduced in size.

Using the Monochrome Version

Single colour printing — The logo must reproduce in black, though tinted paper can be used. The logo 'Positive A' is for use against a white background or tinted paper. The logo 'Negative A' is for use against solid black ink. Against a tint of black the panel versions 'Positive B' or 'Negative B' must be used.

Background colours — When the colour version is unsuitable (e.g. there are colour clashes or a limited amount of colour), the positive logo can be used with flat coloured backgrounds. The tint areas of the logo must reverse out of the background and not overprint the colour. Panel versions of the logo must be used with patterned or halftone backgrounds.

Using the Colour Version

Flat background colour — The logo can be used without panel against flat colour backgrounds provided:
a. it is clearly legible
b. it does not clash with the colour of the background.

Halftone backgrounds — The logo must be used with a panel against halftone backgrounds to ensure that the logo is clearly legible. Where there is an area of flat colour (i.e. there is no discernable pattern in the background), the colour version of the logo without panel may be used provided that:
a. it is clearly legible
b. it does not clash with the background.

Note that the logo when used without panel has to bleed from the top edge.

Correct use against printed colour, logo reverses out of background colour.

Incorrect use against printed colour, logo overprints background colour.

Correct use on tinted paper, logo has to overprint background.

Correct

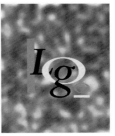

Incorrect position and use.

Correct

Correct use of coloured panel version.

Incorrect position and use of logo against halftone background.

Correct position and use against flat colour background.

Size

Specially-drawn versions of the logo are available for small use reproduction, the minimum size being 12mm square. These versions can also be reproduced at a larger size when poor quality printing techniques are used, for example flexo printing and newspaper advertising (see page 50).

Typefaces

The two typefaces:
Sabon (the typeface used in the logo), and
News Gothic
are to be used on all literature produced by the company. They can be used separately or together in the same document.

The following weights of typeface are acceptable:
Light, Regular and Bold.
Italic, Condensed and Expanded forms can be used but must not appear as part of the formal identity.

Formal Identity

This consists of:
The Logo
Company Name
Company Details

The Logo – can appear separate from the company name only if the company name appears elsewhere in the same document.

Company Name – must appear in black and be typeset in News Gothic Bold, capitals only. FICTITIOUS LOGO LIMITED must appear in one line. The abbreviation LTD can be used where space is restricted. Interletter spacing can vary with individual layouts but should not be less than track 40 (0.2em of the typesize).

Company Details – address etc, must appear in black or red and be typeset in the medium weight of News Gothic in either all caps, or upper and lowercase characters. Interletter space to suit layout.

Type should not go above the top of the 'L'.

FICTITIOUS LOGO LTD (track 40)

Examples of the variety of layouts possible using the guidelines for the Formal Identity.

Type must align with vertical bar.

Note the minimum gap permitted between the logo and the company name.

FICTITIOUS LOGO LIMITED
(track 60 or 0.3em)

FICT

A4 Letterhead

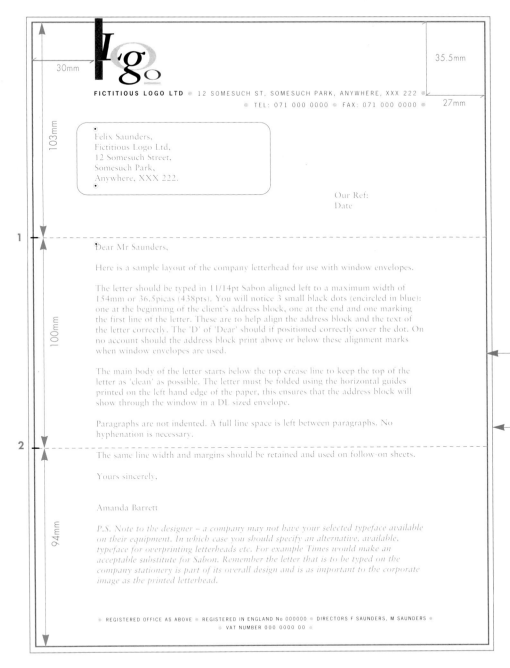

Type Specification for Company Name and Details:
8/16pt News Gothic Bold and Regular, bullets are set in Zapf Dingbats and coloured 30% black. Type aligns right and is spaced (track 40) to fit a measure of 155mm.

Window Envelopes
Address must fall between the printed alignment points (encircled in blue).

Folding Guides 1 & 2
Letter must be concertina folded along the guides indicated so that the address panel appears uppermost.

Trimmed Page Size
Finished size is A4 (210mm wide x 297mm deep).

Bleed Area
Artwork must allow for logo to bleed at top edge.

Type Specification for Registered Company Details
6/11.5pt News Gothic Regular (bullets in Zapf Dingbats), centred on 155mm width. Interletter spacing = track 35 (0.175em).

Colours
Prints in red PMS 1795 and black.

Note
Elements shown in cyan are for information only and do not reproduce.

Follow-on Sheet and Compliments Slip

Follow-on Sheet
The logo is positioned as the main letterhead but is reduced in size by 20%. No company name or details appear on this sheet.
The cyan rectangle denotes the area available for overprinting the text of the letter.

Compliments Slip Type Specification
'With Compliments' is set in 10.5pt News Gothic Bold spaced to fit a measure of 90mm. The company name and details are set in 8/16pt News Gothic Bold and Regular respectively (bullets set in Zapf Dingbats) aligned left to a measure of 155mm.

Compliments Slip Trimmed Size
1/3rd A4 (210mm wide x 99mm deep).

Paper Specification
The letterhead, follow on sheet and compliments slip all print on 100gsm white wove paper.

30mm

42mm

26mm

First line of text 11/14 pt Sabon aligned left to max line length of 154mm.

30mm

L·g·o

WITH COMPLIMENTS

39mm

11mm

FICTITIOUS LOGO LTD ● 12 SOMESUCH ST, SOMESUCH PARK, ANYWHERE, XXX 222 ●
● TEL: 071 000 0000 ● FAX: 071 000 0000 ●

Window Envelope and Business Cards

20mm

Window Envelope
The logo aligns with the edge of the window. The logo size is the same as that used on the follow-on sheet.

Envelope Finished Size
DL size – 220mm wide x 110mm deep.

5mm   40mm   42mm

FELIX SAUNDERS
Managing Director

FICTITIOUS LOGO LIMITED
12 SOMESUCH ST, SOMESUCH PARK, ANYWHERE XXX 222
TEL: 071 000 0000 · FAX: 071 000 0000

ENVELOPES

When overprinting envelopes with a company logo, the logo must be positioned well away from the stamp or franking mark. As a general rule no image should appear below the last line of the address. With specialised postal services, e.g. reply paid mail, there are strict rules governing the design of the envelopes and defined areas for advertising. Contact the relevant postal service for further information.

BUSINESS CARDS

In the business community the landscape format is the preferred layout for business cards for the simple reason that they fit into card files with the information reading the correct way round. Similarly folded business cards are not popular when the essential information is split up, as this means that the card has to be removed from a holder in order to read it.

The size of business cards varies so in order to ensure that they will fit in a card holder their dimensions should not exceed 55mm x 90mm.

Business Card Type Specification
Name: 9/12pt News Gothic Bold spaced to fit measure of 40 mm.
Position: 8/12pt News Gothic Regular track to match spacing used on the name.

Company name: 6/12pt News Gothic Bold spaced to fit measure of 40mm.
Company details: 6/12pt spaced to fit measure of longest line 81.5mm.

Business Card Finished Size
90mm wide x 55mm deep.

Business Card Paper Specification
300gsm white wove card.

A4 Fax Header and 2/3rds A4 Order Form

Logotype
The small use logo at 70lpi must be used (see page 50).

Type Specification
Company name, tel. numbers & fax heading: 11.5/19pt News Gothic Bold spaced as address. Company address: News Gothic Regular spaced to fit longest line 168mm.
Fax Details: 10.5/18.5pt News Gothic Regular. 1pt rules and dotted rules step and repeat at 9.8mm and print black.

Type Specification for Order Form and Invoice
Company name and details: 7/14pt News Gothic Bold and Regular, bullets Zapf Dingbats 30% black. The type is spaced to fit the measure of 155mm. Invoice details: 7pt News Gothic Regular. Forms are designed for use as continuous stationery and for overprinting by the company's laser printer. Pre-printed details are spaced to allow for a constant line drop of 12pts for overprinted information (cyan crosses denote fixed line drop).

Fax form

FAX MESSAGE

FICTITIOUS LOGO LTD
● 12 SOMESUCH STREET, SOMESUCH PARK, ANYWHERE, XXX 222 ●
● **TEL 071 000 0000 ● FAX 071 000 0000 ●**

TO	DATE
FAX NO	NO OF PAGES
FROM	
MESSAGE	

Order form

30mm

ORDER 0000

FICTITIOUS LOGO LTD ● 12 SOMESUCH ST, SOMESUCH PARK, ANYWHERE XXX 222 ●
● TEL: 071 000 0000 ● FAX: 071 000 0000 ● COMPANY REG No 0000000 ● VAT No 000 0000 00 ●

The Sign Maker,
Address etc,
36 Someother Street,
Somesuch Park,
Anywhere,
XXX 222.

YOUR JOB NO   19/VG 009   DATE   12. 12. 98

QUANTITY	DESCRIPTION	PRICE	VAT	DELIVERY
	Perspex signs from layouts supplied Match Pantone colours PMS 288 & PMS 323	798.00	139.65	To address above Not later than 24. 12. 98

NAME Felix Saunders	TOTAL	VAT TOTAL	TOTAL AMOUNT
SIGNATURE	798.00	139.65	937.65

This order is subject to our Standard Purchase Conditions shown overleaf

Invoice

30mm

INVOICE   0000

FICTITIOUS LOGO LTD ● 12 SOMESUCH ST, SOMESUCH PARK, ANYWHERE XXX 222●
● TEL: 071 000 0000● FAX: 071 000 0000● COMPANY REG No 0000000● VAT No 000 0000 00●

Clients Name,
Address etc,
21 Somesuch Street,
Somesuch Park,
Anywhere,
XXX 222.

ACCOUNT NO VG 009   DATE 12. 2 .99

JOB NO	DESCRIPTION	PRICE	VAT	VAT %	TOTAL
XX13	Designs for new factory signage	690.00	120.75	17.5	810.75
XX14	Signage for factory exterior including installation	1,867.00	326.72	17.5	2,193.72

		TOTAL PRICE	TOTAL VAT	INVOICE TOTAL
		2,557.00	447.47	3,004.47

TERMS STRICTLY 30 DAYS NET

Paper Specification
The paper weight for order forms and invoices should not exceed 70gsm and be suitable for use as continuous stationery and overprinting by a laser printer.

Invoice and Order Form Colour Specification
Both forms print in 2 colours: red PMS 1795 and black. There is a 30% tint of black used on the logo, the bullets and dotted lines. The order form also has a dotted line printed in 30% red PMS 1795.

Window Envelopes
DL size window envelopes are to be used with order forms and invoices. The forms are designed to be folded in half so that the address block falls within the window area of the envelope.

FORMS PRODUCED 'IN HOUSE'

Increasingly elements of corporate stationery are being produced 'in house'. If a company's requirement is not large, forms are generated as and when required. This can be achieved through the company's existing computer facilities and database programs, by utilising the company's printed letterhead and then overprinting it with the relevant information.

Alternatively, many database programs have the facility to create custom forms. The logotype can be scanned and saved in a format which allows it to be pasted directly into a form layout which can then be saved as a template. For quality and efficiency this should be output on a laser printer.

8 Page Newsletter
Published quarterly, Signature is posted out to clients, potential customers and employees countrywide. It informs on projects in progress and new developments in sign technology and systems.

Masthead
The artwork for the masthead 'Signature' is available in EPS or Tiff formats.

Type Specification
Text: to be set in 9/14pt Sabon justified to the column width of 65.5mm or ranged left to the narrower measure of 42mm. Headings: to be set in News Gothic Bold aligned left or centred size to be determined by the page layouts, i.e. depending on the available space. Refer to sample layouts. Subheads: 12/14pt News Gothic Bold caps only, a line space is left before each subhead. Captions: to be set in 9/14pt Sabon Bold Italic aligned left.

Cover Photo Area
Photos can use the two, three or four column width.

Note: all measurements are in mm

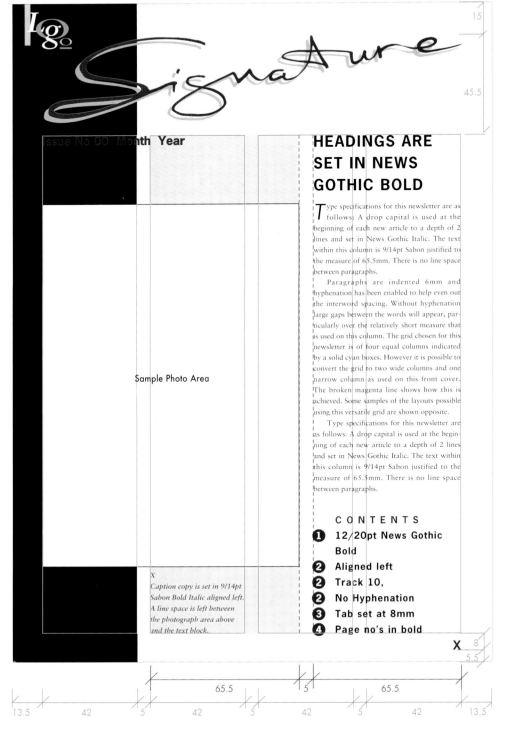

Logo

Signature

Issue No 00 Month Year

Sample Photo Area

X
Caption copy is set in 9/14pt Sabon Bold Italic aligned left. A line space is left between the photograph area above and the text block.

HEADINGS ARE SET IN NEWS GOTHIC BOLD

*T*ype specifications for this newsletter are as follows: A drop capital is used at the beginning of each new article to a depth of 2 lines and set in News Gothic Italic. The text within this column is 9/14pt Sabon justified to the measure of 65.5mm. There is no line space between paragraphs.

Paragraphs are indented 6mm and hyphenation has been enabled to help even out the interword spacing. Without hyphenation large gaps between the words will appear, particularly over the relatively short measure that is used on this column. The grid chosen for this newsletter is of four equal columns indicated by a solid cyan boxes. However it is possible to convert the grid to two wide columns and one narrow column as used on this front cover. The broken magenta line shows how this is achieved. Some samples of the layouts possible using this versatile grid are shown opposite.

Type specifications for this newsletter are as follows: A drop capital is used at the beginning of each new article to a depth of 2 lines and set in News Gothic Italic. The text within this column is 9/14pt Sabon justified to the measure of 65.5mm. There is no line space between paragraphs.

C O N T E N T S
1 12/20pt News Gothic Bold
2 Aligned left
2 Track 10,
2 No Hyphenation
3 Tab set at 8mm
4 Page no's in bold

15
45.5
X 8
5.5

13.5   42   5   42   5   42   5   42   13.5
65.5   5   65.5

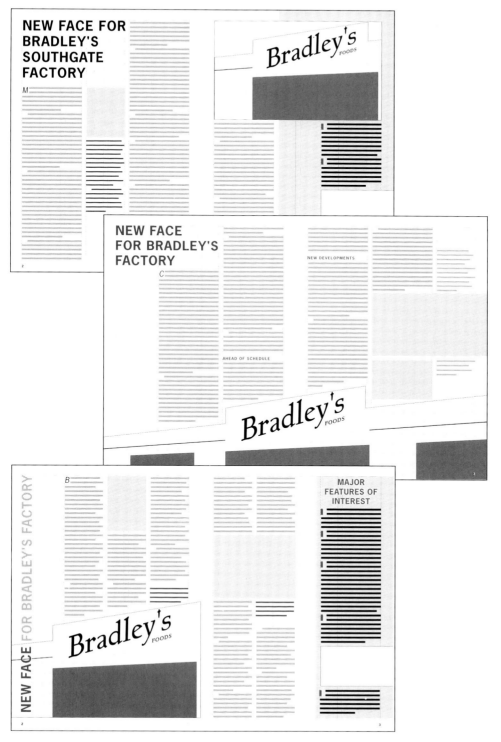

NEW FACE FOR BRADLEY'S SOUTHGATE FACTORY

NEW FACE FOR BRADLEY'S FACTORY

NEW DEVELOPMENTS

AHEAD OF SCHEDULE

Bradley's FOODS

NEW FACE FOR BRADLEY'S FACTORY

Bradley's FOODS

MAJOR FEATURES OF INTEREST

Sample Layouts

A range of possible layouts are shown opposite. These are a guide to using the newsletter grid. Where possible, photographs should be contoured, and type runaround the irregular shape created by the photograph. This helps to add interest to the page. Illustrations and diagrams should be given a similar treatment.

The objective of our newsletter is to present useful information in a lively and attractive format.

Colour Specification

Text: must appear in 100% solid black only. Bold text can be used against tinted panels of black or red.
Captions: print 100% red Pantone 1795.
Headings: print solid black, solid red or tints of either colour.
Subheads: print solid red or black only.

Logotype

The artwork used for this logo has been modified to enhance the quality of reproduction at screen rulings of under 100lpi and at small sizes from 20mm square down to the minimum size of 12mm square.

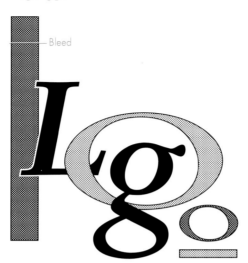
Bleed

QUALITY OF REPRODUCTION

Where an advertisement is placed is of paramount importance, as it governs the quality of reproduction. For some newspapers a screen finer than 80lpi will fill in. With a logo that uses tints, as does the one featured in this style manual, extra care has to be taken that the logo artwork will reproduce well. This involves re-drawing the logo and applying the correct screen ruling for the size of reproduction. The artwork for this re-drawn logo can sometimes be used as the small size logo.

ADVERTISEMENT COSTS

Adverts are costed on the following basis: number of columns x depth (usually in centimetres). This generally results in companies selecting the smallest size possible and then cramming in the maximum amount of information, resulting in the logo appearing too small and the type becoming difficult to read. This is a false economy since the object of advertising is to convey your message as effectively as possible.

Positive A

Note the unacceptable loss of definition when the normal positive version of the logo is reproduced at a screen ruling of 60lpi.

Positive A/S

Is the re-drawn black and white logo artwork for use when screen rulings of less than 100lpi are required. It is also to be used for small size reproduction.

A screen ruling of less than 60lpi is not permitted as the size of dot on coarser screens is too big. The example opposite uses a 30lpi screen.

60lpi

70lpi

80lpi

90lpi

100lpi

Positive A

Positive A/S

Small Use Logotypes

Examples of the minimum permitted size for logo reproduction, 12mm, are shown opposite.

Screens of 60lpi are only acceptable at this size for laser printing and should not be used for commercial reproduction unless the logo is sized at 15mm or above.

The recommended screen rulings for newspaper advertising are 70lpi to 90lpi, depending on the quality of the paper.

For magazines and brochures a minimum of 100lpi is recommended.

Advertising Formats

MINIMUM
HEADLINE
12PT

MINIMUM TEXT SIZE
7.5PT WITH 3PTS
LEADING
MAXIMUM LINE LENGTH
MUST LEAVE AT LEAST
1 EM AT FULL CAP
SIZE CHARACTER
SPACE EITHER SIDE OF
TEXT BLOCK.

071 000 0000
• • • • • • • • • • • • • • • •
FICTITIOUS LOGO LTD
12 SOMESUCH ST,
SOMESUCH PARK,
ANYWHERE, XXX 222

Type Specification
Headline: minimum 12pt
News Gothic Regular or
Bold caps and small caps
centred or aligned left,
leading and track to fit.
Text: not less than
7·5/10·5pts News
Gothic Regular or Bold
caps and small caps
centred or justified,
minimum horizontal
scale 90%.
Phone No: not less than
7.5pt Bold caps to
appear directly above
company name.
Address: not less than
5pt News Gothic Regular
or Bold full size capitals,
can appear in text block.
Company name: not less
than 5pt full size capitals
track to fit maximum
width, must appear after
dotted rule at base of
advert.

MINIMUM
HEADING SIZE
12PT

MINIMUM TEXT SIZE 7·5PT WITH
3PTS LEADING. MAXIMUM LINE
LENGTH CALCULATED BY LEAVING
A SPACE OF AT LEAST 1EM
HEADLINE FULL CAP SIZE
BETWEEN LOGO AND TEXT BLOCK
AND AT LEAST 1EM TEXT
FULL CAP SIZE SPACING
BETWEEN TEXT BLOCK AND RIGHT
HAND BORDER.

TEL: 071 000 0000
• •
FICTITIOUS LOGO LIMITED
12 SOMESUCH ST, SOMESUCH PK, ANYWHERE XXX 222

**Single Column
Format**
Logo 20 x 20mm
Note: on all
advertisements use the
logotype version Positive
A/S at 70lpi to 90lpi for
reproduction in
newspapers.

**Double Column
Format**
Logo 19 x 19mm
**Three Column
Format**
Logo 20 x 20mm

ADVERTISING DESIGN

An average advert can contain a company logo,
name, address, phone/fax numbers, together with
a contact name if relevant. All this and there must
still be enough space for the message.
It is not surprising that the most precious
commodity in advertising is also the rarest to be
seen – space. The company image is strongly
reflected in its advertising. A logo is noticed in a
newspaper *whether or not* the reader is interested
in the actual content of the advertisement at the
time they see it. Subconsciously they may even
form an opinion about a company from its
advertising. Leaving space within an advertisement
separates it from the clutter surrounding it, drawing
the eye of the reader. To test an advert design
paste it in to a typical page taken from the
targeted publication.

MINIMUM HEADING SIZE 12PT

MINIMUM TEXT SIZE 7·5PT WITH 3PTS LEADING. MAXIMUM LINE
LENGTH CALCULATED BY LEAVING A SPACE OF AT LEAST 1EM
HEADLINE FULL CAP SIZE BETWEEN LOGO AND TEXT BLOCK
AND AT LEAST 1EM TEXT FULL CAP SIZE SPACING BETWEEN
TEXT BLOCK AND RIGHT HAND BORDER.

TEL: 071 000 0000
• •
FICTITIOUS LOGO LIMITED
12 SOMESUCH ST, SOMESUCH PK, ANYWHERE XXX 222

Sample Newspaper Advertisements

Sample Layouts
The overall proportions of the sample advertisements on this page should be used as a guide to the desired shape. Column widths will vary from publication to publication.

SIGNS FOR A GREAT FUTURE!

YES THINGS ARE LOOKING UP, SO GET YOUR COMPANY NOTICED. AT FICTITIOUS LOGO WE OFFER YOU EXPERTISE GAINED FROM 12YRS AT THE FOREFRONT OF SIGN TECHNOLOGY. TAKE ADVANTAGE OF OUR

FREE CONSULTANCY SERVICE
071 000 0000
••••••••••••••••••
FICTITIOUS LOGO LTD
12 SOMESUCH ST,
SOMESUCH PARK,
ANYWHERE, XXX 222

Single Column Sample Advertisement
27mm wide x 12 cm deep

Double Column Portrait Sample Advertisement
57mm wide x 9.5 cm deep

Double Column Landscape Sample Advertisement
57mm wide x 3.5 cm deep

SIGNS FOR A GREAT FUTURE!

YES THINGS ARE LOOKING UP. NOW IS THE TIME TO GET YOUR COMPANY NOTICED. AT FICTITIOUS LOGO WE OFFER YOU EXPERTISE GAINED FROM 12YRS AT THE FOREFRONT OF SIGN TECHNOLOGY, PHONE OUR

FREE CONSULTANCY SERVICE
ONE OF OUR EXPERIENCED SALES STAFF WILL COME AND ASSESS YOUR NEEDS, OFFER ADVICE AND PREPARE A COMPETITIVE QUOTE.
TEL: 071 000 0000
••••••••••••••••••••••
FICTITIOUS LOGO LIMITED
12 SOMESUCH ST, SOMESUCH PK, ANYWHERE XXX 222

SIGNS FOR A GREAT FUTURE!
12 SOMESUCH ST
SOMESUCH PARK
ANYWHERE XXX 222
071 000 0000
••••••••••••••••••••••
FICTITIOUS LOGO LIMITED

Three Column Landscape Sample Advertisement
90mm wide x 6 cm deep

ADVERTISING STANDARDS

Standards governing the content and form of advertising vary from country to country. Direct response advertising and direct mail often have strict guidelines governing the content of promotional literature as well as press advertising. Contact the relevant associations for further information.

SIGNS FOR A GREAT FUTURE!

YES THINGS ARE LOOKING UP. NOW IS THE TIME TO GET YOUR COMPANY NOTICED. AT FICTITIOUS LOGO WE OFFER YOU EXPERTISE GAINED FROM 12YRS AT THE FOREFRONT OF SIGN TECHNOLOGY, PHONE OUR

FREE CONSULTANCY SERVICE
ONE OF OUR EXPERIENCED SALES STAFF WILL COME AND ASSESS YOUR NEEDS, OFFER ADVICE AND PREPARE A COMPETITIVE QUOTE.
TEL: 071 000 0000
•••••••••••••••••••••••••••••••••••
FICTITIOUS LOGO LIMITED
12 SOMESUCH ST, SOMESUCH PK, ANYWHERE XXX 222

Buildings

FICTITIOUS LOGO LTD

The vertical red bar must be positioned to run from the top of the brick work (or cladding) where it joins the eaves.

Signage of our premises has two functions:
● to clearly identify our property.
● guide visitors and staff around the premises safely and efficiently.

The main factory sign must include the corporate logo and company name. The sign is to be fixed directly to the front elevation of the building through the use of back fixings. The wall should be painted in magnolia smooth exterior paint.

The logo and company name have a three dimensional effect achieved through the method of fixing:
● The red components of the logo (the vertical bar and small letter 'o'), are flush with the wall.
● The black letter 'L' is set 100mm proud of the wall.
● The grey large 'O' and horizontal bar is set at 200mm.
● The black 'g' at 300mm.
● The company name is set at 100mm.

Method of Fixing
Back pins are to be used to fix the metal letters to the wall. Male back fixings are glued or screwed into the back of the letters. The corresponding female fixing is screwed into the wall.

Entrance ➡
⬅ Goods In
No Entry

PLANNING PERMISSION

It is essential to ensure that the planning permission has been sought and granted by the relevant authorities before fixing signs to the exterior face of a building.

Directional signs are set in News Gothic Bold upper and lowercase. Signs are fixed to the walls at a constant distance of 30mm. Note: prohibitive and warning signs are coloured in the corporate red.

Vehicle Livery

Logo Position for Side Panel of Transit

Red bar aligns with the top sill of the van. Left side of van: logo sits within the back panel as shown above. Right side of van: Logo sits in front panel. The company name must be positioned to allow for the sliding door.

Logo Position for Rear of Transit
The logo sits below the left hand rear window. The company name is centred along the horizontal moulding to the rear door.

VINYL SIGNS FOR VEHICLES

There are several methods that can be used to apply logos and text to vehicles. The most commonly used include: signwriting by hand, transfers and vinyl lettering. For all methods, check with the sign maker how the artwork should be presented – as this varies according to the type of equipment the company uses.

Vinyl signs are cut from rolls of different coloured vinyls. The range of colours can be limited so check that the sign maker has a satisfactory match for your selected colour. There are several grades of vinyl available based upon the lifespan of the substrate. e.g. seven year, five year and three year. For vehicles the seven year life span is preferable, bearing in mind that a vehicle is subjected to sun, rain and snow in addition to the rigors of a car wash. Modern day vinyls will go over mouldings and panels of a vehicle, but take these into account when positioning a logo and lettering.

Fictitious Logo Limited has a small fleet of vehicles consisting of white Ford Transits. The livery has been designed to appear on both sides of the vehicle and the back. The front of the vehicle is left plain.

The vehicles represent a mobile advertisement and should be well maintained, reflecting the image of a caring and efficient company.

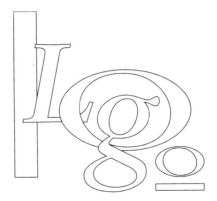

Keyline Logo Artwork
The special keyline artwork can be used to facilitate easy scanning and colour separation for company signage.

The following projects have been selected
to illustrate corporate design in action.
From the initial rough ideas of the designer
through to the finished product, they show
how a particular design solution is
reached.

Each of the projects are prefaced by a
company profile and design brief with the
intention that they may be used as practice
assignments by the student of design.
For the company manager responsible for
commissioning design work, they provide a
valuable insight into the content of a
design brief and the way a job is
progressed through to finished product.

All of the projects are based on actual
design jobs undertaken by the author. The
briefs and the design solutions are real, as
are the problems encountered along the
route between the two!

PROJECT 1

THE BRIEF: TO DESIGN A LOGOTYPE WHICH WILL BE USED ON STATIONERY, PROMOTIONAL LITERATURE AND SIGNAGE.

Client and Job Profile

The Office of Major Projects is a government department of the State of Victoria, Australia. Its responsibilities include overseeing and promoting development projects within the State.

Lynch's Bridge, 'Melbourne's Newest Suburb' is part of a major project to develop land once used for stock grazing and sale yards. It is situated on some of the highest land close to the city of Melbourne, overlooking the Maribyrnong River.

The architectural style for this residential development is in sympathy with the surrounding suburb of Kensington. The houses have pitch roof lines, gable ends and verandahs. There are in addition to the housing, parkland, a bike and walking reserve and a formal garden. This is a prestigious development covering a large area of land. The identity for the project should reflect both the quality and attractiveness of the development.

CLIENT	Office of Major Projects, Melbourne, Australia.
JOB NAME	Logotype Design for Lynch's Bridge.
DESCRIPTION	Design a logotype for use on stationery, promotional literature and signage for the Lynch's Bridge site.
PURPOSE	To create a versatile logotype and style guidelines for both colour and monochrome reproduction.
COLOURS	Three colour, two colour and single colour version required. Reproduction will be in both Pantone and process colours.
COPY	The words 'Lynch's Bridge' should appear as part of the logo.
VISUALS	Colour visuals of all colour versions.
FINISHED ART	Master artwork in EPS format on disk. Bromide masters of monochrome version.
DELIVERY DATE	To be advised.
SPECIAL COMMENTS	Architect's plan of the proposed residential housing is attached to this briefing form.
	This is a prestigious, quality development and the overall design should reflect this. It should show the style of housing and if possible include some visual reference to the river and parkland that are part of the site. Bear in mind that this logotype must be suitable for reproduction on large banners or billboards surrounding the development site.

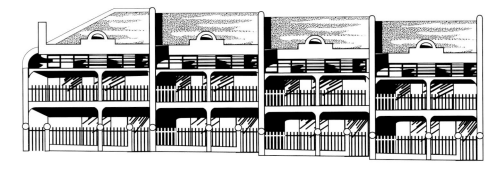

Initial roughs are crude, the elements look thrown together. Individual elements need to be refined and simplified. Shown opposite are just two of the stages of the initial design roughs for the logotype.

Attention is focused on the name and in particular the emphasis of each word. First they are given equal emphasis.

Lynch's Bridge

Later visuals give more impact to the word Lynch's.

As discussed at briefing stage this logo can consist of four elements:

● the name
● the buildings
● the river
● the parkland.

There is quite strong visual reference for the buildings in the form of the architect's plans, so the designer first looks at how the other elements can be represented and combined. The aim is to achieve a strong composition of the elements. Initial roughs take the form of pencil sketches, through which it soon becomes obvious that the elements must be simplified, the tree is reduced to an outline and the river is symbolized by horizontal rules.

It is important to emphasize the key elements of the logo – the name and the building – so further roughs work on the correct balance of these two elements.

Taking the name first the decision is made to emphasize the word 'Lynch's' over the word 'Bridge'. This gives the name more impact, but the typography seems weak.

The terraced buildings under construction at Lynch's Bridge reflect a style which was popular in Melbourne around the turn of the century. The typography of this period would have included some quite ornate hand cut typefaces and the face selected for 'Lynch's' has a similar feel although the typeface – Bertie was actually designed in the nineteen-eighties by Alan Meeks. To contrast with the ornate face of 'Lynch's', Futura Bold is selected. By juxtaposing the two typefaces a feeling of the old and the new is achieved which accurately reflects the development plans for the site.

The river is indicated by the horizontal rules and the solid bar, the word bridge reverses out of the bar – the bridge across the water.

The building is added to the typography, and the decision is made to leave the tree out of the logo. The single building looks good with the typography but has the impression of an establishment rather than a housing development. So two buildings are used. (This is a good decision as it turns out there is a restaurant in Melbourne called Lynch's!).

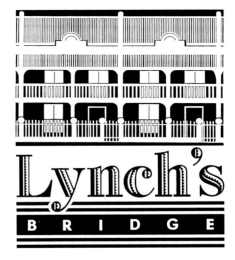

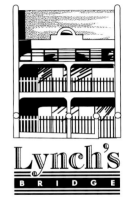

The plans of the buildings are re-drawn and simplified, and a master artwork of the logo is drawn up by hand and then scanned and saved as a TIFF image.

It is a requirement of the design brief that the logo should be versatile – that it can be used in both monochrome and in colour. Different versions of the monochrome design are examined and an alternative positive version of the logotype is designed using a 70% tint of black. This version is a good match to the colour versions (see following page) and is the preferred version for monochrome reproduction.

Left, two positive black and white versions of the logotype are designed, one for line reproduction and the other having a 70% tint of black in addition to the solid black.

As the reversed out form of the logo does not look good a panel version is designed for use against dark backgrounds, which are defined as those with a 40% tint of black and above.

Far left, a negative version of the logo does not look good, so a panel version, left, is to be used against backgrounds of 40% black or darker.

Some colours clash with the logo, while others can affect its legibility. Guidelines have to be drawn up governing the usage of all versions of the logo – the corporate style manual.

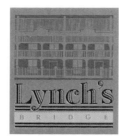

The final choice of colour for the logotype will affect colours on all literature produced by a company. As some colours will not sit happily next to each other, the designer has to make the decision to avoid using them with the company logo, or change the colour of the logo. The latter option is not recommended, as changing the colour of the logo will lessen the impact of the image.

Right, the three colour version of the logotype uses burgundy, grey and blue. The blue is replaced by grey in the two colour version.

The primary objective of this logo is to gain recognition for the project and the last thing the designer wants is for this image to become muddled and possibly confused with other projects. Consequently the two and three colour versions of this logo both use the same colour – burgundy and grey, the three colour version adds a light blue used to highlight the water area.

Grey has been deliberately chosen as one of the colours for these logos as it can be made up from a tint of black. Black provides the best contrast against white paper for text setting on leaflets and brochures, which means that a two-colour leaflet can print in black and burgundy, and still reproduce the two-colour logo – the grey being made up from 70% black.

Below, the preferred monochrome version uses a percentage tint of black matching the grey used in the colour versions.

Mercury

Client and Job Profile

The client is a specialist tour operator to Malta. The parent company is looking to establish a new tour company for the Mediterranean island and its sister island Gozo.

The new company has been registered under the name Mercury Holidays. It will be offering mid-range hotel and apartment accommodation in Malta together with flight packages from England.

Already having a thorough knowledge of the marketplace in which it operates, the company wants to create a new image that reflects its aim of an efficient, reliable service. This is especially important at a time when some tour companies have collapsed, in some instances leaving tourists stranded.

Consequently, it is vital that the corporate image projects a feeling of reliability and confidence in the services offered.

THE BRIEFS:
1. TO DESIGN A CORPORATE IMAGE FOR A NEW TRAVEL COMPANY.
2. DESIGN A HOLIDAY BROCHURE USING THE NEW IMAGE.

CLIENT	Mercury Holidays, London, England.
JOB NAME	Corporate Identity.
DESCRIPTION	Design logotype for use on stationery range: a) letterhead, b) compliments slip, c) business card (bear in mind possible further usage on tickets, baggage labels and promotional items).
PURPOSE	To establish a consistent image to be used throughout company literature. Letterheads to be overprinted with a letter or holiday itinerary by client using their own laser printers.
FORMATS	Letterhead A4 portrait to fit ordinary DL envelope (not window envelope), fax header A4 portrait, compliments slip 210mm wide x 99mm deep (=1/3rd A4), business card 90mm wide x 55mm deep.
COLOURS	Maximum of three colours.
COPY	Company name, address, telephone, fax number and Telex number, AITO logo.
VISUALS	Client would like to see more than one design solution for logotype. Colour visuals of final selected design on stationery range.
FINISHED ART	To be advised.
COMMENTS	Logotype to reflect aims of efficiency and reliability, but still retain a 'holiday feel'. Largest proportion of holiday makers tend to be in the mid-age range late 30s to early 60s. Holiday packages offered for mid-range budget.

By looking at the various tour company images in the visually busy environment of high street travel agents, three things become apparent:

● Companies are referred to by a single name – e.g. Thomson, Sunmed. This is the strongest element of the logo, often depicted in a typeface that has been specially drawn or modified for the company.

● The symbol, although often used together with the company name, assumes an interpretive role. For example, conveying the images of sun and sea, or colours associated with the country of destination.

● Simpler images are more memorable and stand out better when taken in the context of a travel agent's window or a rack of glossy brochures.

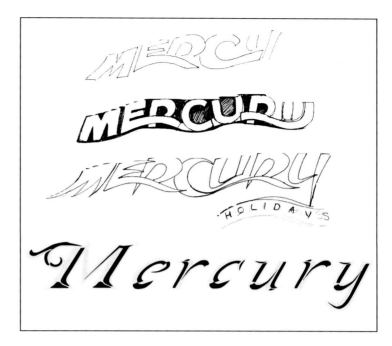

Mercury – winged messenger.
Further pencil roughs start to work on the alternative associations of the winged messenger. Messenger has the wrong connotations but the wing provides a good symbol for a travel company.

Although this company's literature will be mailed out rather than displayed in a travel agent's window, it must compete with other tour operators and other destinations.

It is important that the name is memorable. Through the use of visual association it is possible to increase the chances of the name being retained. If a symbol is used it must reflect the name Mercury. If the name is used on its own then the lettering style must be distinctive and should reinforce the name.

Mercury suggests two possible images:
● Liquid silver
● Winged messenger

Both these images are explored by the designer and the second option is found to be more representative of a holiday company.

Mercury – liquid silver.
Initial roughs try out ways of making the type flow and mimic the silver quality of mercury. The idea is discarded on two counts:

● The image evokes an automotive feel rather than a holiday atmosphere.
● Cost – we are limited to the four colour process for printing and silver can only be reproduced faithfully using a Pantone metallic ink.

Pencil roughs work on the relationship between a wing symbol and the company name. Care has to be taken that the symbol does not dominate the name. It should be acting in a supportive and interpretive role.

Below you can see how the designer moves towards the solution that is shown opposite.

This solution allows the wing to dominate too much. It is also too busy – the elements are competing with one another. However, it certainly posesses one of the key ingredients – a lively feel.

The final image on the pencil roughs shown above is worked up more fully using the computer. The wing is constructed in a draw program and the type is set in Parisian, then joined to a semi-circular path. The word 'holidays' is drawn by hand and scanned at 600dpi this was saved as a TIFF image. The whole logo was then combined and the colours were added to achieve the final visual shown opposite.

MERCURY
H O L I D A Y S

The logo needs to be simplified and have greater legibility. A less complicated solution is reached by adapting the wing shape used in the previous logo and returning to an idea from earlier roughs. The colours are reduced to just two. Red and black are selected as they provide a strong contrast and will reproduce well against light backgrounds – for example, light blue skies of a sunny holiday resort.

The result, shown above, has a better balance between the elements. The company name is the most prominent element – the wing actually forms part of the lettering and does not appear as a separate element. 'Holidays' is given the least emphasis, as it follows the same angle of the larger lettering but is in a much smaller typesize. Overall the logo is clearly legible and it is a good solution to submit to the client.

Continuing work on the wing symbol, a more informal approach is tried. A loose form emerges using two wings to form a bird shape. In these roughs, shown opposite, the wing has again tended to be the dominant element. The format of the fourth rough is worth developing, though the wing has to be scaled down in proportion to the company name. In addition, a way of rendering the wings to give a loose, fluid feel has to be found.

The logo shown above could be made up in a number of computer programs which have the ability to skew type horizontally. The typeface for Mercury, Century Schoolbook, has been skewed to an angle of 26°. The same angle is used to tilt the word 'holidays'. The letter 'M' is converted to paths, then split so that part of the letter can be removed and the drawing of the wing logo positioned over the missing section.

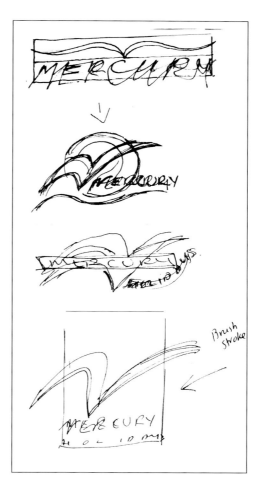

Brush stroke

By tilting the red rectangle the elements in the design are drawn together. The rectangle is to be used bleeding off the the top of the page.

The black-and-white version uses a 20% tint of black on the wing symbol and an 80% black tint on the panel.

Using a paint brush and black ink, a suitable symbol for the wing is drawn. This is then scanned and saved in bitmap form at a resolution of 600dpi. This resolution is sufficient to pick up the slight ink splatter of the brush while at the same time keeping the image a solid black.

The type was drawn at an earlier stage of the design roughs, but matches the wing well – the 'r' forms almost the same shape as the wing symbol.

The elements are linked by the red panel and their proportions are adjusted to give more emphasis to the company name.

Finally, the red panel is tilted at an angle of 20° and the word 'Holidays' typeset in Bodoni Bold and sized to fit the width of the panel. A drop shadow in black is added and a thin keyline runs round the original type, now coloured yellow. This ensures that it will reproduce well against light colours – including white which will be the paper colour for company stationery.

This is the version the client approves; it now has to be incorporated into company stationery and appear on a sales brochure.

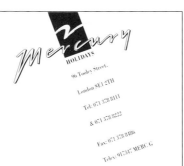

The logo is positioned over to the right and bleeds off the top of the letterhead. This leaves maximum space for the recipient's address. The top fold line (shown in cyan) is clear of the last line of the address.

The compliments slip follows the same format as the letterhead. The words 'with compliments' are set at an angle of 20° to match the address.

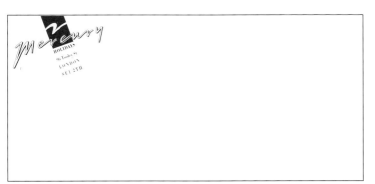

CLIENT	Mercury Holidays.
JOB NAME	Holiday brochure using new Corporate Identity.
DESCRIPTION	Glossy holiday brochure with three intro pages, ten accommodation pages with photos and descriptions of hotels and apartments. For Booking Form and Price List existing layouts will be used as a separate insert (four pages bound into the centre of the brochure). Designs are not required for these.
PURPOSE	To obtain holiday bookings through displaying the services offered by the company, together with the accommodation in an attractive, clear easy-to-read format.
FORMAT	A4, 16-page self-cover (i.e. uses same paper as the inside pages).
COLOURS	Four colour process.
COPY & PICS	*Front cover (page 1):* 1 large and 1 small inset photo. Logo. Destination heading – Malta and Gozo. Contents headings – Hotels and Apartments, Holiday Complexes, Flights Only. Special Offer – Children Travel Free. *Pages 2 & 3:* a) The AITO quality charter: approx 240 words detailing the advantages of booking a holiday through a member of the Association of Independent Tour Operators + AITO logo, b) 10 headed paragraphs on services offered e.g. climate, transfers to hotel, airport etc., approx 60 words each, c) Page by page contents, d) Free offers 190 words + 4 headings and finally climate chart *and* leave space for 3 photos! *Page 4:* a) Map of Malta & Gozo, b) 1 paragraph profile of the islands, c) Description of Malta and Gozo and main resorts plus photos. *Accommodation pages:* 2 or 3 properties a page each property consists of: a) Name, rating expressed as stars, resort name, b) Descriptive copy approx 100 words, c) Key facilities e.g. cocktail bar & restaurant, games room etc., d) No. of rooms, no. of lifts, no. of floors, tel no.
VISUALS	Pages as listed above.
COMMENTS	This is a real challenge – to design a publication where so much and such a variety of information is included!

The volume of copy on pages 2, 3 and 4 of this job does not allow room for much space. It requires a highly versatile grid that can accommodate different blocks of text yet also maximize the amount of space available.

The client has previously produced brochures where every inch of the page has been filled with either text or photographs and coloured tints. This has been a tried and trusted format for travel brochures for many years. The Thomson Freestyle brochure broke the mould in the eighties and other companies since have produced distinctive designs. But the majority still prefer to get as much information as possible into a given space.

Mercury were prepared to try a more open format for the accommodation pages and a grid was designed for the brochure which could be applied to both the busy introduction pages and to the more open accommodation pages.

This grid, based on five equal columns, is shown opposite. On the introduction pages, single and double columns are used to break up the text into different sections. The AITO charter is extremely important, given the much publicised failure of a number of holiday companies – consequently it is positioned at the very beginning of the brochure and highlighted through the use of a coloured background panel.

A five column grid is used for both intro and accommodation pages. Elements are added to the page which will be moved around until a satisfactory layout covering the double page spread is achieved.

The panel behind the folios has been copied from the logo and adds an element of continuity to the pages, reflecting the corporate style. The heading typeface is Bodoni, which was used for the word 'holidays' on the logo.

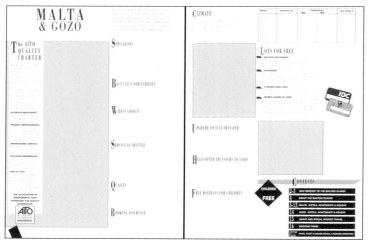

The final balance of elements is achieved. The main body of text fills the central four columns of the double page spread, leaving the three columns either side for smaller elements and colour photos.

The accommodation pages, have more space, giving a lighter feel than the intro pages. The five-column grid works well for both the pictures and the text.

The facilities offered by each property in the accommodation pages are laid out separately from the main descriptive text. This has to be easy to read, as many people will choose a specific accommodation for its facilities.

Finally, the cover is designed. The logo is centred and bleeds off the top of the page. The photograph selected has a large blue sky area which provides the perfect background to the logo and inset panel.

3

PROJECT

THE BRIEF : TO
DESIGN A
CORPORATE
IMAGE FOR A
BUSINESS CENTRE
INCLUDING
SIGNAGE AND
ASSOCIATED
PUBLICITY
MATERIAL

Client and Job Profile

A Business Development Centre is being set up in the Suffolk town of Bury St Edmunds. The centre will provide support in the form of professional advice and information for small to medium enterprises throughout the West Anglia region. Here the main business support agencies from the region will pool services, resources and skills under one roof. Each of these agencies have their own corporate identities so the image of the centre must be such that it can be used alongside pre-existing logos.

A premises has been found which offers a window frontage to the street. This will be utilised for small displays, but will need some form of signage announcing the West Suffolk Business Development Centre.

CLIENT	West Suffolk Business Development Centre.
JOB NAME	B D C Corporate Identity.
DESCRIPTION	Identity for new Business Centre. To include: logotype, stationery range, signs for the premises.
PURPOSE	To present a memorable and interesting identity that will encourage visitors to the centre. Logo must be adaptable for advertising in various publications, including local newspapers. Also, it is to be used as a window sign which will be produced using vinyl lettering. Identity must be able to co-exist with the logos and colours of the various enterprise agencies using the centre, as joint publicity ventures may be required.
FORMATS	Usual stationery range based on A4 letterhead.
COLOURS	Maximum two colours
COPY	West Suffolk Business Development Centre, the additional words 'Linking Business' should accompany the logo. Address: 2 Looms Lane, Bury St Edmunds, Suffolk, IP33 1EZ. Telephone: 0284 760206, Fax: 0284 767157, Free Phone: 0800 387575.
VISUALS	Full colour visuals required for letterhead, compliments slip and business cards. Visual showing suggested signage to front of premises.
BUDGET	This whole project has largely been funded through sponsorship from business within the area. The budget is tight. All signage and promotional material has to be economical to produce, utilising one and two colours where possible.
COMMENTS	The Business Development Centre is similar to a shop in that it should have a strong presence in the street. It has an open plan design for easy access for businesses, owner managers and personnel from larger companies. A photo of the premises is shown with this brief.

This centre should look as attractive as possible as its corporate image is closer to that of a retailing outlet than a business consultancy. The individual enterprise agencies will be projecting their own established images within the 'business shop' and will provide the professional credibility underpinning the centre's image.

The actual premises, pictured on the preceding page, is on four levels including the basement, with large window areas. Its potential for advertising the services of the centre should not be overlooked. The left hand ground floor window will be used for small window displays which change from month to month, so an area must be left free for this. The window size is approximately 2.5m square.

All the above should be taken into account when designing the logo. In addition, the logo should reproduce well in black and white for advertising and single colour brochures.

The logo's of the four main organizations using the Business Development Centre.

The logos of the other organizations using the centre are shown above.

West Suffolk Business Development Centre is a bit of a mouthful. In general conversation it is referred to as the Business Development Centre. The catch phrase 'Linking Business' is not part of the formal identity, and should these words be dropped in the future it should not affect the rest of the logo. Where a long name like this is chosen, it is essential to analyse

These design roughs show some of the difficulties presented by the length of the name. Some design solutions work well for the words Business Development Centre, but run into trouble when the other elements are added.

its components and if possible emphasize the key words.

The triangle is a good symbol for the centre, the top angle forms a roof shape symbolic of the centre – being the roof under which various services are gathered. However, problems are encountered when trying to integrate the words, so another approach is tried, taking the theme of development. The progression from dark to light, negative to positive, sums up the aim of the centre to develop businesses.

A shape emerges that unites the key words with the regional classification – West Suffolk – while at the same time achieving the correct emphasis between the two. The background effect needs a lot of work. Bearing in mind that this logo has to be read on a window and also be legible in a newspaper advert, the background is of crucial importance. It is easier to create a precise effect on the computer, where the colour characteristics of the typeface can be matched against different backgrounds.

Only through experimentation can the correct background effect and balance of typefaces be found. The first attempts, although effective, were dismissed. (Can't you just see somebody emulating this effect by chucking a brick through the window!).

The third solution is strong but the progression from dark to light is too sudden.

A steady progression from dark to light is achieved through using a tint in the fourth solution. This has potential.

Right, the image is shown at original size. The custom screen was specified as: screen type round dot, screen angle 45°, screen ruling 30lpi.

The same image is reduced to 50%. Note how the screen remains the same.

The line screen, shown opposite, was made up from a single element consisting of three corner points; this was then cloned and moved to achieve the correct spacing. The whole group of lines were then rotated to 45°.

Finally a black and white master logo is drawn up for small scale reproduction. The words 'Business Development Centre' have been set in bold type, this ensures that the characters will not fill in when reproduced at a small size.

Using a customized screen (i.e. a screen other than the default setting) that has been generated by the computer can cause a few problems, particularly when you decide to scale your image up or down in size. The image will change all right but the screen may have to be re-specified or it will retain the same line ruling (lpi) as the original image.

For ease of reproduction as well as aesthetics, the final effect chosen for the background was based on a line screen at an angle of 45°. The screen was made up in a draw program (in this case Aldus FreeHand). The type was set in Helvetica and New Century Schoolbook.

The words 'Linking Business' have been deliberately placed so that they can be removed at a later date if required without re-drawing the whole logotype. The yellow rule would remain to provide a strong base for the logo.

2 LOOMS LANE
BURY ST EDMUNDS
SUFFOLK IP33 1EZ

TEL: 0284 760206
FAX: 0284 767157
FREE PHONE:
0800 387575

The final colours used for the logo were: Pantone blue 286 and yellow 109. These colours were selected for the strong contrast between them. They stand out well on signage and on promotional literature.

2 LOOMS LANE
BURY ST EDMUNDS
SUFFOLK IP33 1EZ

TEL: 0284 760206
FAX: 0284 767157
FREE PHONE:
0800 387575

WITH COMPLIMENTS

PETER ALDER

Business Information Manager

2 LOOMS LANE, BURY ST EDMUNDS,
SUFFOLK IP33 1EZ

TEL: 0284 760206
FAX: 0284 767157
FREE PHONE: 0800 387575

Managed by the Mid-Anglian Enterprise Agency Ltd. Registered in England No: 1805308
In conjuction with the Chambers of Commerce, Suffolk International Trade Centre and Suffolk Training and Enterprise Council.

The frontage of the building has a high proportion of window area. The main activities of the business centre will take place on the ground floor, with an open plan information centre/office area. The top two floors will contain a function room for training and other offices yet to be allocated. This makes the main area of focus the ground floor.

2.4m

2.4m

2.4m

1.88m

1.88m

2.2m

Main Window

Entrance Door

Main Window

This will be used for small exhibitions that will change every month. Enough open window space must be left for these.

Entrance Door

This is set back and not immediately obvious from the road. It consists of double doors with glass panels in the top two thirds.

External Signage

Planning permission is needed for signs erected on the perimeter of the property. This also applies to signs on the external walls.

There needs to be a freestanding sign at street level. This sign should include the Business Centre logo plus the founding members names and/or logos (see page 76). The names are as follows:

- Mid Anglian Enterprise Agency Ltd
- Chambers of Commerce
- Suffolk Training & Enterprise Council.
- Suffolk International Trade Centre.

These names must appear in full, or alternatively, the logos can be used.

Style for Window Lettering

The type is set in Helvetica Medium 80% condensed in yellow with a drop shadow in blue as used on the logotype. The use of the drop shadow ensures that the words are legible against both light and dark backgrounds.

The main window sign is placed high up to leave the full width of the window free for displays. The typeface with drop shadow is used again on the remaining ground floor windows to advertise the services of the centre. This also helps to draw in the casual visitors to the centre.

The main notice board uses the participating company names only. They are aligned with the baselines of the words 'Business' and 'Centre'. Space is left for an additional company name, which may be added at a later date.

There is a door that faces you as you come up the first flight of steps to the centre. This could be mistaken for the main entrance door which is up a further flight of steps to the right. A sign is placed on this door to direct visitors. Again the drop shadow is used to ensure that it is easy to read and in addition the arrows set in Zapf Dingbats have been added to direct visitors up the staircase to their right.

Style for Notice Boards

The typeface is the same as that used for the windows – Helvetica Medium condensed to 80%. The drop shadow is not necessary for notice boards as the background will always be white.

Possible confusion over the entrance to the centre is averted by the sign placed on the door pictured left. The actual entrance doors are up some stairs to the right. Again the drop shadow is used for the lettering. The arrows set in Zapf Dingbats are chosen to match the style of the Business Development Centre's logo.

The spiral of copy was specifically written to fit the design of the front cover. The need to show the front of the building and also emphasize that it is a centre for business advice – open to all – were united in this design.

The interior of the leaflet uses the two corporate typefaces used on the logo – Helvetica and Century Schoolbook.

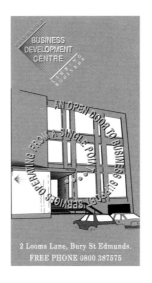

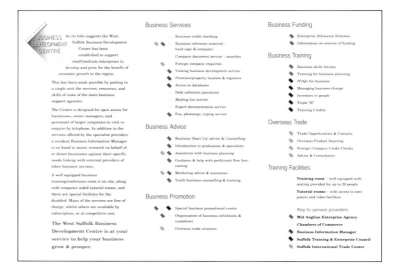

In the first promotional brochure it is important to establish three key factors:
● the identity of the centre,
● the location of the centre and
● the range of services offered.

The logotype is used wherever possible to help establish the identity and act as a point of recognition for further publicity.

An illustration of the premises figures prominently on the front cover – as does a map on the back to establish firmly its location.

The services offered at the centre are highlighted by coloured 'flags', these double as a key to the individual agencies providing the relevant service.

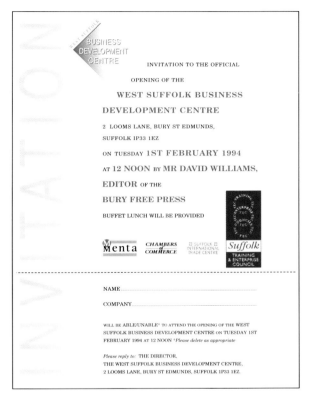

Further promotional material produced in the same corporate style begins to establish the identity of the Centre, and the official opening is packed out!

The invitation and newspaper advertisement announcing the opening of the Business Development Centre have a similar format.

The black and white version of the logotype is used in the newspaper advertisement and reproduces well. There are two recommended typefaces for use on all Business Development Centre publications – Helvetica or Century Schoolbook. The Helvetica is selected for the newspaper advertisement as it reproduces more cleanly on newsprint, particularly when used at small sizes. The more formal typeface – Century Schoolbook is used on the invitation.

4

PROJECT

THE BRIEF: TO
PRODUCE A
DESIGN FOR A
TECHNICAL
BROCHURE
WITHIN THE
CONSTRAINTS OF
AN EXISTING
CORPORATE STYLE

Client and Job Profile

The State Electricity Commission of Victoria is responsible for the maintenance and supply of power to the Australian state of Victoria.

In addition to its above responsibilities, the SEC runs an Energy Business Centre. This centre is dedicated to providing information and giving practical demonstrations to businesses on the most cost-effective use of electrical energy. One of the ways in which the Centre provides information to businesses is through the production of brochures and information leaflets. To maintain a common style for these publications, the SEC set up a comprehensive set of guidelines. Every leaflet and brochure designed for the Business Centre must be designed within the constraints of these guidelines ... *the corporate style.*

CLIENT	The State Electricity Commission of Victoria, Melbourne, Australia.
JOB NAME	Quality of Supply – Problems, Causes and Solutions.
DESCRIPTION	Technical brochure outlining the nature of possible disturbances to electrical power supply. Primarily for business users, but could be of interest to some domestic users of electricity.
PURPOSE	To provide easy access of information to users of sensitive electrical equipment. The brochure will be posted out in response to requests for information, displayed at exhibitions and displayed in the reception area of the Energy Business Centre.
FORMAT	A4 portrait.
NO. PAGES	32 plus 4 page cover. **COLOURS** Full colour cover, 32 page - 2 colour.
ILLUSTRATIONS	1. Reference photos supplied by client are not for reproduction. An illustration style based on the photos needs to be developed. Alternatively, black and white photos can be taken. 2. Diagrams need a consistent style.
COPY	Copy will be supplied on floppy disk (3.5 in., in Microsoft Word).
VISUALS	Full colour visual of front cover, and double page spread.
PROOFS	Laser prints of whole brochure.
FINISHED ART	To bromide only with colour mark up. (Colour separations by printer).
COMMENTS	Needs the illustrations and diagrams to liven up text. Text should be presented so its easy to look up and to pick out sections. Clean/authoritative overall feel.

All information produced for the SEC Energy Business Centre must use the corporate style designed specifically for brochures and other literature produced by the centre. A copy of the style manual would be given to the designer at the time of the briefing. The following is a synopsis of the relevant sections from the manual.

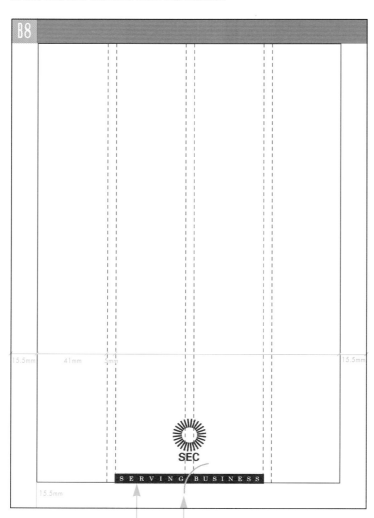

Coding Square

The letter categorizes the brochure (in this case B for Energy Business Centre). The letter must be typeset in 36pt Univers 49 Light Ultra Condensed caps.

The number distinguishes it from other publications from the Energy Business Centre, and is set in 36pt ITC Century Book Condensed - further condensed 15%. There must be 1mm letter spacing between the characters. The two or three characters are centred within the 15mm square box with 3mm spacing top and bottom within the square.

The square prints in solid Orange PMS 021 (shown here in 50% magenta + 90% yellow). Characters reverse out white.

Top Strip

Size:15mm deep trimmed size.
Colour: either PMS 321 (shown here as process colour 100% cyan, 30% yellow and 20% black), or solid grey PMS 424 (65% black).

SEC Logo, Graphic Symbol and Panel

These must appear centred with the baseline of the panel aligning with the baseline of the grid. Colours as shown opposite. If they are to be used against a dark background, the SEC logo and panel should reverse out white. The type within the panel prints grey. The graphic symbol representing the category of brochure must appear in orange.

Panel   Graphic Symbol

The grid for the inside pages of the brochure is the same as that used on the cover. The top colour strip is omitted on the inside pages.

The Typeface

The typeface can be any from the Univers range and/or any from the Century range.

The Colours

A full list of permitted colours is given with the style manual, which is too long to include here. So for the purposes of this project, assume that any colour is permissable.

Sample Spread

Using the four column grid you have the option of running type to 1, 2, 3 or even the full 4 column width. The layout below uses the two column width.

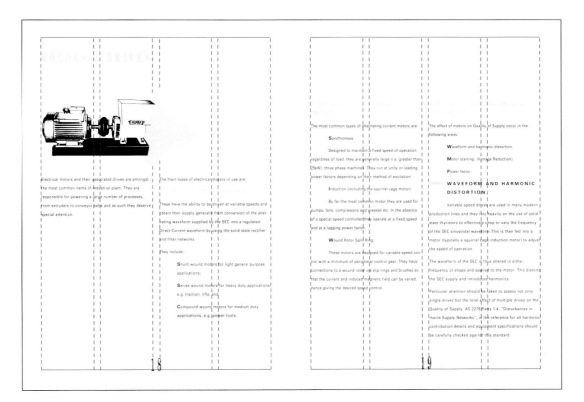

Illustration

The illustration uses the photograph from the briefing sheet. It has been converted to line (all the mid-tones have been dropped out). The background has been cut out – a clipping path was drawn around the required image area which was then saved together with the image as an EPS file. The file was then imported into the desk top publishing program where the background shape was added and brochure text typeset.

With technical brochures you often get a variety of headings and subheadings, and this brochure is no exception. The first thing to do after reading the copy is to assess how many different headings there are and set a style for each. The individual styles can be saved on style sheets in most DTP programs and allocated function keys – this allows you to access a specific style with a keystroke. If you change your mind at a later date it is easy to change all the headings by re-specifying the style.

Below is a sample of copy taken from the brochure text.

Chapter 7, Motors & Drives.

Effects of Motors on Quality of Supply.
The effect of motors on Quality of Supply occur in the following areas:-

Waveform and harmonic distortion
Motor starting. (Voltage Reduction)
Power factor

Waveform and Harmonic Distortion
Variable speed drives are used in many modern production lines and rely heavily on the use of solid state thyristors to effectively chop or vary the frequency of the SEC sinusoidal waveform.

7
MOTORS & DRIVES
EFFECTS OF MOTORS ON QUALITY OF SUPPLY

The effect of motors on Quality of Supply occur in the following areas:

Waveform and harmonic distortion.

Motor starting. (Voltage Reduction).

Power factor.

WAVEFORM AND HARMONIC DISTORTION

Variable speed drives are used in many modern production lines and rely heavily on the use of solid state thyristors to effectively chop or vary the frequency of the SEC sinusoidal waveform.

Above is the same text as it appears in the brochure (the size of type and leading have been proportionally reduced to fit the narrower column width of this book).

The word 'chapter' has been edited, leaving the numeral alone to define the section – while the title is moved to make a second line.

Heading 1 ('Effects of ....') has three sub headings, the initial letters of which are set in the same size and colour as the corresponding headings which follow. As these following headings are also subheads of Heading 1, they are indented and a horizontal bar is added to provide a colour link with their parent heading.

A potentially dull brochure can be livened up through the creative use of charts and diagrams. Even when colours are limited, you can use interesting textures or symbols to add a bit of life. However, it does take time and a lot of jobs do not have budgets that allow for a lot of experimentation. The key point to remember is that the chart should be easily interpreted and understood.

An example of one of the tables from the brochure is shown below. The 4-column grid is used to size the panels dividing up the chart's categories. Blocks of coloured tints are used to divide the table instead of vertical and horizontal rules.

Type of supply system	Supply system voltage at point of common coupling (kV)	Total harmonic voltage distortion U percent	Individual harmonic voltage distortion percent	
			Odd	Even
Primary and Secondary distribution	Up to and including 33	5.0	4	2.0
Transmission and Subtransmission	22, 33 and 66 110 and above	3.0 1.5	2 1	1.0 0.5

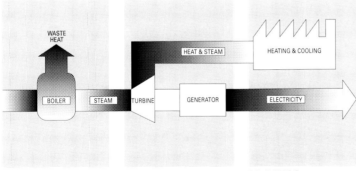

FUEL   **ELECTRICITY**   **PROCESS**

This diagram appeared in a previous brochure on Cogeneration. It was originally reproduced in two colours – burgundy and SEC grey, using graduated tints with a coarse line screen (shown here at 85lpi) to denote the progression of the heat generated.

With full process colour the same diagram is reproduced using graduated tints. The screen ruling has been reset to default. This means it is reproduced at the screen ruling used for this book. The diagram was drawn in Aldus FreeHand.

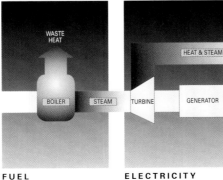 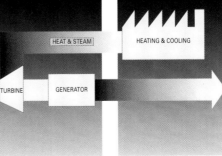

FUEL   **ELECTRICITY**   **PROCESS**

The front cover is designed using the specifications shown at the start of this project. A dramatic photograph of lightning is chosen for use on the cover. The colour of the photograph is so intense that the picture is enlarged for maximum effect. The photograph is positioned carefully, the lightning bolt avoids running through either the SEC logo or the 'Serving Business' panel.

The typeface used for the heading is New Century Bold, horizontally scaled to 35% and spaced to fit the width. It is shown here in 19pt but its actual size is 42pt.

The subhead has also been set in New Century Bold, but has not been horizontally scaled. Shown here at 8pt, its actual size is 18pt.

The SEC logo and 'Serving Business' panel are reversed out of the background colour. The versions in grey can only be used against white or light backgrounds.

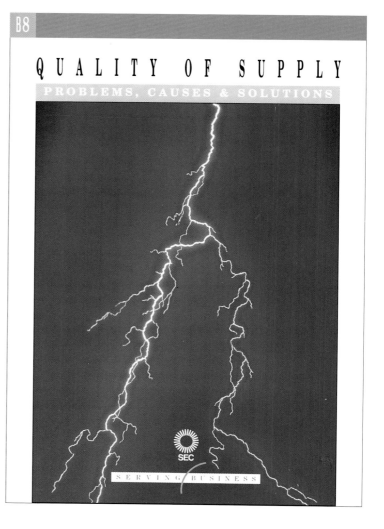

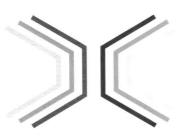

C1

C O G E N E R A T I O N

ENERGY EFFICIENCY AND AN
ENVIRONMENTALLY ACCEPTABLE
ALTERNATIVE

SEC

SERVING BUSINESS

Other covers produced
for the Energy Business
Centre using the
corporate guidelines.

E7

LOW COST WATCHMAN
SECURITY LIGHTING

SEC

SERVING BUSINESS

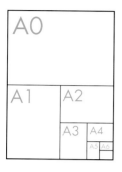

A Sizes The international paper sizes listed below:

Sheet size	Millimetres	Inches
A0	841 x1189	33.1 x 46.8
A1	594 x 841	23.4 x 33.1
A2	420 x 594	16.5 x 23.4
A3	297 x 420	11.7 x 16.5
A4	210 x 297	8.3 x 11.7
A5	148 x 210	5.8 x 8.3
A6	105 x 148	4.1 x 5.8
A7	74 x 105	2.9 x 4.1

Ascender Top part of lower case letters which rise above the x-height e.g. b d h.

ASCII American Standard Code for Information Interchange, (for Macintosh users: 'Text-only' files). All computers use the ASCII character set, which means text can be exchanged between computers. Text online services such as CompuServe use ASCII and can be accessed using any computer equipped with a modem.

Alignment How images or text align on a page. For text setting there are four pre-set options: aligned left, aligned right, justified or centred.

Baseline Imaginary horizontal line upon which the base of a character sits.

Baseline Shift Typesetting aid allowing individual characters or groups of characters to be set above or below the normal baseline.

Bit Short for binary digit – the smallest unit of computer storage. A bit can represent one of two states: 1 (on) or 0 (off).

Bitmap Images stored as a series of bits, can have a ragged appearance – like an image drawn on graph paper where squares are filled in either black or white.

Bleed Images on artwork that extend beyond the trimmed edge. Sometimes printed colours that overlap each other are said to bleed.

Bromide Light sensitive photographic paper used to output hard copy from imagesetters used for artwork in preference to film.

Bullet The symbol •.

Camera Ready Artwork Flat artwork that is ready to be shot by a repro camera or scanned in order to produce the final films used to make printing plates.

Cap Height The distance from baseline to the top of a capital letter.

Centre Spread Pair of pages in the middle of a publication that form a single sheet of paper.

Centred Referring to text where all lines are aligned from a central point. See *alignment.*

Characters Upper and lowercase letters, numbers and punctuation marks that comprise a type font.

CMYK Cyan, magenta, yellow and key (black), the four colours used in the process colour method of printing.

Coated Refers to paper that has a china clay finish. Colours printed on this surface react differently to those printed on uncoated paper. Using the Pantone colour system a 'C' is included after the number of the colour to denote coated paper.

Colour Separation Preparation of coloured artwork whereby it is divided into the relevant colours ready for making the individual printing plates.

Continuous Stationery Letterheads, forms etc., that are pre-printed on a long roll of paper rather than individual sheets, used by businesses outputting large quantities of invoices, orders etc, 'in house'.

Contour An image that has had all or part of the background cropped out – also referred to as etched out or cut out.

Copy Literally to copy an image, or used in typesetting to describe the manuscript of a document ready for typesetting and/or formatting.

Cromalin Coloured proofs made up from the film separations. Colours are mixed from powders, then added film-by-film to simulate printed colour.

Crop Marks Lines drawn at the edge of a page denoting the area to be trimmed off after printing, or marks on a photograph showing area that is to reproduce. Also known as trim marks.

Descender The parts of the lower case letters which extend below the baseline e.g. g j p q y.

Dingbat A decorative graphic element, e.g. the characters making up the typeface Zapf Dingbats.

DL Envelope size – 220mm wide x 110mm deep.

Drop Cap The first character in a paragraph set in a larger size and occupying more than one line depth.

Drop Shadow An effect achieved by duplicating an image and offsetting the duplicate behind the original. The colour or shade of the duplicated image is usually changed to give the desired shadow effect.

Dpi Refers to the number of dots per inch that an output device can produce, e.g. a laser printer or image setter.

Em A fixed amount of space, equal to the point size of the typeface you are using. In 12pt type an em space is 12 points wide.

En A fixed amount of space equal to half an em space.

EPS Encapsulated PostScript is a data exchange file format, which allows text and graphics to be exported between programs recognising the EPS format. EPS images can be printed on postscript printers only.

Floppy Disk or Floppies Plastic disk (hence floppy) protected by hard plastic case, used primarily for backing up or transferring computer files and for software distribution.

Folio Page number.

Font or Fount All the characters for one typeface in one weight e.g. Times Bold.

Grey-scale. Method of scanning and storing continuous tone images on computer without using a halftone screen. The quality of the image is determined by the different levels of grey, e.g. 16, 64, 256.

Grid A designed framework used to help position elements accurately on a page. The grid does not print but should be saved along with any type specifications as a template for documents that are regularly up-dated, such as newsletters, catalogues.

GSM or g/m² Grammes per square metre. Used to measure the weight of paper, e.g.100gsm paper is often used for letterheads, 300gsm lightweight card is used for business cards and brochure covers.

Hairline Unit of measurement equal to 0.25pt (0.08mm).

Halftone An image comprising of dots that results from the screening process used to convert continuous tone images into a printable form.

Hard Copy Printed copy of the contents of a computer file.

Horizontal Scaling To expand or condense selected characters without affecting their height.

Hyphenation The process by which words are broken in order to fit within a specified line length.

Imagesetter A high resolution output device for computer images. Outputs an image at a selected resolution to either bromide or film as required.

Indentation Typographic term referring to the positioning of lines of text in relation to preceding or following lines. There are four main types of indent: left indent, right indent, first line indent and hanging indent.

'In House' Refers to material produced within the offices of a company i.e. not using outside services.

Justification Alignment of text in a paragraph whereby the lines of type form straight left and right hand side margins with the exception of the last line of the paragraph.

Kerning Reducing or increasing the space between individual characters.

Laid Type of paper which has a watermark running through it in the form of lines running across the sheet.

Landscape A horizontal page orientation, i.e. the

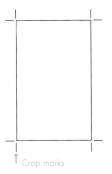

↑ Crop marks

Drop shadow

Grid – three columns

Halftone – magnified to show dots resulting from the screening process.

SCALING

Horizontal scaling

30pt
20pt
10pt

Type size is measured
in points

Portrait   Landscape

60% tint of black screened
at 65lpi

60% tint of black screened
at 100lpi

**OVER-
PRINT**

Overprint – the cyan text
appears green as it
overprints the yellow ink.

Negative

Positive

width of the page is greater than the height. Also referred to as wide.

Layout The arrangement of text and graphics on a page.

Leading The vertical space from one baseline of text to the next.

Letter Spacing Refers to the horizontal space between characters.

Ligature Two or more connected letters, e.g. fi or fl.

Line Art An image made up from black or white elements without using continuous tone.

Lpi Refers to number of dots per inch in a halftone screen. Because the dots are arranged in lines the resolution of the screen is measured as lines per inch.

Machine Proofs Accurate form of proofing whereby a small print run is used to produce printed proofs from the actual printing plates. (This can prove expensive as corrections can involve the re-making of plates).

Margins The white space between each edge of the page and the printed area.

Masthead Title of magazine, newspaper etc.

Measure Typographic term referring to the width of a text block.

Moiré An undesirable pattern on printed halftone colour images, resulting from misregistration or incorrect screen angles.

Negative The reverse of a positive image i.e. dark elements appear light and light elements appear dark.

Object-oriented An image containing multiple bits per pixel, giving a smoother effect than the one bit per pixel of a bitmapped image.

Overprint Where coloured text or an image prints on top of another printed colour.

Pantone® An international standard for colour matching. See *PMS*.

Pica Unit of measurement equal to 12pts.

6 picas = 1inch = 72 pts.

PICT A file format for bitmapped or object-oriented graphics used to transfer images between programs.

Pixel Abbreviation for picture element. The individual display dots that make up a computer screen display.

Plate A specially prepared light sensitive surface which is exposed to the image of an artwork from the colour separated film negatives or positives. After the image has been properly fixed within the surface of the plate, it is inked up in a printing machine and the required amount of copies are run off.

PMS Pantone Matching System®. Colours are often specified using this abbreviated form e.g. PMS 339.

Point A unit of measurement equal to 1/72 of an inch or 0.352mm.

Point of Sale Promotional graphics used to advertise a product at the point of sale, e.g. a shop, garage etc.

Point Size The size of the characters in a font measured from ascender to descender.

Portrait A vertical page, i.e. the depth of the page is greater than the width. Also referred to as tall.

Print run Number of copies to be printed.

Proof A sample of a job used to check artwork or typesetting before continuing on to the final product.

Proofreading Checking proofs of typesetting to spot any errors. Corrections are marked on the proof.

Ranged Left and Ranged Right Same as aligned left and aligned right, see *alignment*.

Registration Refers to the exact positioning of two or more printed colours.

Registration Marks Symbols appearing in exactly the same position on each colour separation, which when printed 'in register' fall precisely one on top of each other.

Resolution Measures the sharpness of an image. In the case of a computer screen, this is measured in pixels per inch, for an output device e.g. laser printer, it is measured in dots per inch.

Reverse Out Where text or an image knocks out the printed background colour.

Run-around Forcing text to run around a photo, other text or a graphic image. The amount of white space between the text and the image is known as stand-off.

Sans Serif Without serif. See *serif*.

Scale To reduce or enlarge an image to a specific size.

Scan To convert an image to a digitized format that can be stored on a computer. In the four colour printing process, to scan is specifically to break down an illustration into the four separate images – separations – which together will re-create the full colour picture.

Screen The means by which a continuous tone image is broken up into a halftone image.

Screen Ruling The size of the screen as determined by the number of lines of dots per inch, see *Lpi*. A coarse screen will have less lines per inch e.g. 60lpi, a fine screen will have more e.g. 200lpi.

Separation One of the four images (cyan, magenta, yellow or black), created when scanning a colour image for four colour process reproduction.

Self Cover A publication which uses the same paper stock for the cover as that used for the inside pages, allowing the publication to be printed as one job, i.e. the cover does not have to be printed separately.

Serif The small finishing strokes that cross the ends of the main strokes that form a character.

Set Solid Text that has been typeset solid, i.e. without the use of additional leading.

Set Width The pre-set width of characters in a typeface.

Skew To slant an element vertically, horizontally or in both directions.

Small Caps Capital letters whose cap height

equals the x-height of the lower case characters in the same typeface.

Stock The paper or card specified for a job to be printed upon.

Style Sheet Used to specify text, line, colour etc for a particular job. Saved with the document or template as required.

Template A file format that, once saved, cannot be overwritten. Used to store grids, typographic and colour specifications for documents which are frequently updated such as newsletters and catalogues.

Text Wrap Similar to runaround. Text is flowed around a graphic image.

Tracking Reducing or increasing the space between selected characters. Generally applied to blocks of text as opposed to kerning which is applied to pairs of characters.

Trapping Overlapping colours, in order to prevent gaps appearing between them when elements are printed slightly out of register.

TIFF Tagged Image File Format. Bitmapped file format particularly useful for scanned images, able to represent colour and grey scale images at virtually any resolution.

Tint A percentage of any colour, including black.

Wove Smooth-surfaced paper, having no watermark or pattern, used in preference to some laid papers that are unsuitable for laser printing.

x-height The height of a typeface's lowercase letters, excluding ascenders and descenders.

Registration marks (misregistered)

Registration marks (in register)

REVERSE OUT

Reverse out– the cyan text knocks out the background yellow ink.

SKEW

Text skewed horizontally

CAPS CAPS

18pt capitals and small caps

Trapping: un-trapped colours (top image) and trapped colours (bottom image).